BS
2506
.Y68
1997

W9-DJE-007

PAUL
THE JEWISH
THEOLOGIAN

A Pharisee among Christians, Jews, and Gentiles

BRAD H. YOUNG

HENDRICKSON
PUBLISHERS

GOSHEN COLLEGE LIBRARY
GOSHEN, INDIANA

BS
2506
.Y68
1997

PAUL
THE JEWISH
THEOLOGIAN

© 1997 by Hendrickson Publishers, Inc.
P. O. Box 3473
Peabody, Massachusetts 01961–3473
All rights reserved
Printed in the United States of America

ISBN 1–56563–248–6

First Printing—November 1997

Library of Congress Cataloging-in-Publication Data

Young, Brad.
   Paul, the Jewish theologian: a Pharisee among Christians,
Jews, and Gentiles / Brad H. Young.
   Includes bibliographical references and indexes.
   ISBN 1–56563–248–6 (pbk.)
   1. Paul, the Apostle, Saint. 2. Pharisees. 3. Judaism—
Regulations—Christianity. 4. Christianity and other
religions—Judaism. I. Title.
   BS2506.Y68 1997
   225.9′2—dc21   97–2478
                                                                CIP

The Scripture quotations contained herein are from the *Revised Standard Version of the Bible,* copyright © 1949, 1952, 1971 by the Division of Christian Education of the National Council of the Churches of Christ in the U.S.A., and are used by permission. All rights reserved.

This book is affectionately dedicated,
with much appreciation, to my parents,

Senator John W. and Claudeen Humes Young

Table of Contents

Acknowledgments

Paul the Jewish Theologian: A Pharisee among Christians, Jews, and Gentiles is the product not only of my own writing and research but also of numerous conversations with friends and colleagues. I highly value the insight of scholars who have contributed to my understanding of Paul.

The mysteries of Paul's teachings are locked away in his culture and historical context. I am deeply indebted to my mentor, Professor David Flusser of the Hebrew University in Jerusalem, who has shaped my understanding of Paul and his theology. I treasure his friendship. His original thought and creative genius offer fresh perspective. Shmuel Safrai has also helped immensely in my research of Second Temple period Judaism. Dr. Robert L. Lindsey offered new approaches to unraveling some of the more complex issues of Pauline theology. I continue to mourn Dr. Lindsey's untimely death on May 31, 1995.

Joseph Frankovic read and edited the entire manuscript. His work improved the style and argument. I value his editorial gifts and his outstanding scholarship. Joseph made significant suggestions, helping greatly in the process of interpreting Paul's message and comparing his teachings to those of ancient Judaism.

My friends David Bivin and Dr. R. Steven Notley have encouraged me throughout the writing of the book. I have appreciated the opportunity to discuss Paul's epistles with them. Dr. Notly's doctoral dissertation at the Hebrew University has broken new ground in understanding pre-Pauline

Christianity and Paul's innovations. Dr. Marvin Wilson and Dwight Pryor have interacted with me on Paul's view of the Torah and early Christian interpretations of Paul. I have enjoyed discussing Paul with Dr. Roy Blizzard, who has challenged me to dig deeper into the primary sources. Dr. Ron Mosley has helped me in the research effort.

I have benefited from being able to discuss Paul with my friend Rabbi Leon Klenicki. I appreciate the input I have received from friends involved in Jewish-Christian dialogue such as Rabbi Arthur Kahn, Rabbi Marc Boone Fitzermann, Rabbi Charles Sherman, and Sheila Mudd. My experiences with the Ecumenical Theological Research Fraternity in Israel assisted me in isolating the special problems of Pauline studies. My friend Malcolm Lowe has helped me define and resolve issues more decisively.

My colleagues at Oral Roberts University, Dr. Jerry Horner, Dr. Howard Ervin, Dr. Robert Mansfield, Dr. Trevor Grizzle, Dr. David Dorries, and Dr. Tom Mathew have all been sources of insight and encouragement. Founder and Chancellor Oral Roberts has encouraged building bridges of friendship and reconciliation with the Jewish community. I appreciate the emphasis on academic integrity and spiritual maturity at the School of Theology.

I have benefited greatly from friends working with me through the Gospel Research Foundation. Dr. John Swails, Barry Chambliss, Tim Eckbald, Jim White, Linda Weaver, Pat Young, John Mark Young, and Gayle Young Brazil have been of tremendous help in the process of writing the book. David Reed worked diligently in proofreading the text and preparing the indexes. My parents, Sen. John W. and Claudeen Humes Young, as well as my son, Matthew David, have given much support. It gives me great joy to be able to dedicate this volume to my parents.

I must express my gratitude to Dr. Burton Visotzky and Dr. Cheryl Brown for writing the forewords to the book. Dr.

Brown's experience in Israel and love for the Jewish people affect the students in her courses. Rabbi Visotzky has taken time from a arduous schedule to write a foreword which challenges Christians and Jews to work together for a more meaningful relationship in the future. I appreciate the authenticity of his scholarship and his effort to foster textual research. His books, like *Reading the Book: Making the Bible a Timeless Text* and *The Genesis of Ethics,* have challenged readers to embrace the study of the sacred text with a fresh awareness of its message and a spiritual perception of its meaning.

The rabbis taught that every verse possesses seventy faces. Hence there are numerous ways to interpret each text of Scripture. Surely Paul's teachings have caused intense debate because of the rich diversity of interpretations. Paul will continue to stir up controversy. Nonetheless, placing Paul firmly within the stream of Pharisaic thought, interacting with Christians, Jews, and Gentiles, must offer much-needed fresh perspective. Here I must gladly say a heartfelt thank you to many friends who have contributed to the writing of this volume. I hope that it will be a stepping-stone for increased sensitivity and awareness of Paul's historical situation as we explore the force of Paul's original message.

Foreword

*Rev. Dr. Cheryl Anne Brown**
Professor/Consultant
Theological Assistance Group
European Baptist Federation

The title of Brad Young's new book, *Paul the Jewish Theologian*, to many—both Jews and Christians—may be an oxymoron, an impossible combination of two mutually exclusive categories. Although Paul was born a Jew and trained as a Pharisee, he is viewed as the person who single-handedly transformed the provincial Palestinian Jewish Jesus movement into a world-wide church that early separated from its Jewish roots and became almost exclusively Gentile in faith and practice. In the process of this transformation, certain affirmations of Jesus himself had to be sacrificed in order to make Christianity more appealing to non-Jews. Such affirmations included Jewish nationalism and Torah observance, teachings basic to Judaism though expendable to Paul in his quest to spread his new faith throughout the known world. Consequently, Paul rather than Jesus is often referred to as the founder of Christianity. I remember the first time I heard this as a graduate student in Israel from a Jew who had a deep appreciation for Jesus as a good Jewish prophet who sought to bring renewal to the faith

---

*Cheryl Anne Brown is the author of *No Longer Silent: First-Century Jewish Portraits of Biblical Women* (Louisville, Ky.: Westminster/John Knox, 1992).

of his own people. That was the first of countless times I have heard and read the same idea from Jews and Christians.

Christians have been influenced to accept this view by a generation of New Testament scholars who worked from an important presupposition of form criticism: the New Testament accounts of Christian origins reveal several strata of development, one a Palestinian Jewish stratum, the "primitive church in Jerusalem," and the other a Hellenistic stratum. Paul was regarded as the leading shaper and interpreter of the latter. Scholars have posited a linear development from the earlier to the later stratum. Current scholarship has for the most part discarded this paradigm, rightly concluding that the neat, cut-and-dried categories suggested by earlier scholars never existed. Scholars today recognize that Judaism in the Second Temple period was remarkably diverse both on Palestinian soil and in the Diaspora. So, happily, the straw house has fallen; but lamentably the conclusions have not. In many people's minds, Paul remains the "founder" of Christianity and is cut off almost, if not entirely, from his Jewish roots.

But for me a question has persisted: Is that really true? Does this perception of Paul adequately and accurately take into account the facts in the texts about Paul or by Paul? After wrestling long and hard with these issues I have concluded, along with Brad Young, that a new look at Paul is definitely in order. For this reason, I applaud his careful, insightful analysis of the biblical passages related to the life and teachings of Paul. Too often specialists and non-specialists alike have read these texts from the perspective of later church history or Jewish-Christian relations rather than from the perspective of Second Temple Judaism and Christianity. Brad Young rightly highlights the hermeneutical issues related to such a study, advocating that we recognize the presuppositions we bring to the text and acknowledge how those affect our reading of the text. Also, for too long we have been satisfied with others' conclusions about Paul's doctrine. This includes influential figures such as many early church fathers, who took Paul's teaching another step away from its Jewish roots and led the church to not only see itself as not connected in any way to Judaism, but to see Judaism as the great anti-Christ. They sought to stop Judaism at any price, even to the point of contradicting the teachings of Jesus himself regarding his own people. The resultant history of Jewish-Christian relations stands as a travesty of all that Jesus came to accomplish and is nothing less that a profaning of the name of God.

The need for a new look at Paul's theology from the perspective of his Jewish roots is recognized by biblical scholars engaged in the pursuit of an accurate understanding of both Judaism and Christian origins. A call for such an approach is issued by Victor Paul Furnish in his article on Pauline studies in *The New Testament and Its Modern Interpreters* (Scholars Press, 1989, p. 338):

> . . . I should like to stress the importance of pursuing the question about Paul's relation to Judaism, specifically the question about what kind of Jew he was. . . . When Paul says he had been "as to the law a Pharisee" (Phil 3:5; cf. Gal 1:13–14), that needs to be taken seriously . . . [I]f the advances made in Pauline studies over the past forty years are to prove worthwhile, they must result in some new models according to which "Pauline theology" can be analyzed and presented. The old models . . . did not recognize, or take sufficient account of, the profoundly situational character of Paul's letters. Nor did they attempt, with any seriousness or consistency, to interpret his message in relation to the multiple social, religious, ecclesiastical, and personal forces with which he was constantly and concretely engaged during the whole course of his ministry. The real challenge for interpreters of Paul's thought lies just here: to find ways of respecting the situational and dialogical character of his theology without abandoning the attempt to understand its most fundamental convictions and its most pervasive concerns.

Paul the Jewish Theologian goes a long way toward meeting this challenge. Although certainly others, such as W. D. Davies, E. P. Sanders, Joseph Klausner, Leo Baeck, and J. A. Sanders, have helped to further understanding of Paul as a Jew, Brad Young offers an extremely well-informed, insightful study of Paul as a Jewish theologian. He moves from the starting point of Jewish theology—rather than from Christian theological categories—to the Pauline texts and brings a wealth of background knowledge of both Judaism and early Christianity to his analysis. He is well equipped to speak on these issues, having studied Judaism and Christian origins at the Hebrew University of Jerusalem with the world-renowned Jewish scholar, David Flusser. (Readers will be interested to know that Dr. Young's conclusions about Paul are not entirely shared by his mentor.) Among the many important qualities Brad Young gained from his years of study with Jewish scholars is a love for and an almost exclusive focus upon *the text,* what it actually says and does not say; and this perspective has led him to some new, important, and sometimes "unorthodox" conclusions.

I have had the privilege of knowing Brad Young, first as his teacher and then as a friend and colleague, for more than twenty-five years; I have always been impressed with his rare combination of tremendous intellectual acumen and deep spirituality. Both are given expression in this ground-breaking volume that is certain to give rise to new reflections and new discussions about Jews and Christians and between them. Ultimately it is hoped that this book will promote new levels of mutual understanding and relationship.

Foreword

Rabbi Dr. Burton Visotzky*
Appleman Chair of Midrash
and Interreligious Studies
Jewish Theological Seminary, New York

The Pharisee Saul of Tarsus is arguably one of the most influential religious figures in the history of Western culture. His influence was accomplished by the force of his personality and through his epistles—both those he wrote and those attributed to him. It seems that all who experienced Saul/Paul firsthand were left with a strong and lasting impression. Some who met him became his followers, Christians, while others became his enemies. This latter group was made up of Christians, pagans, and Jews. Those who read his letters but did not know him drew their conclusions without recourse to the author. They, too, seemed either to embrace or vehemently reject Paul's teachings. But those who relied only on the letters often read things into those writings that Paul never intended. And Paul, forceful as he was in person, could not correct misapprehensions made in his absence or after his death.

It was following his death, in the generation after the crucifixion, that Paul's work, represented in his letters and in the Acts of the Apostles, became a central part of the Christian canon, alongside the Gospels. For almost two thousand years

---

*Burton Visotzky is the author of *Reading the Book: Making the Bible a Timeless Text* (Schocken) and *The Genesis of Ethics* (New York: Crown, 1996).

since, Paul's words have been cited as Scripture by believing Christians in support of their ideas or in opposition to their antagonists. The *midrash* done on Paul's works took his own *midrash*, which he wrote on both the Hebrew Bible and the story of Jesus Christ, and turned it into a new, new Torah. This new teaching was truly something different from the Pharisaic Judaism from which Paul sprang. The infusion of hundreds then myriads of Gentiles into the Christian community all but guaranteed that Paul's thoroughgoing Jewish origins would be eclipsed just as were Jesus' own Jewish roots.

The Paul of Christian history is, then, a Paul vastly different from the Pharisee Saul who was born in Tarsus and lived his days first as a student in Palestine and then on the road for Christ. Saul the Pharisee continued to preach Christianity to the Jews, but his successes among the Gentiles assured that Paul the Apostle was regnant. In the end, Saul may well have been an observant Jew who counseled observance for other Jews even as he sought to bring them to Christ. But through his preaching to the Gentiles, to the church outside the circumcision, Paul invented a wholly new religion with Jesus at its theological core. It was then and remains today Christianity.

It is impossible to overlook Paul's accomplishment. It is equally impossible to overlook the hatred and strife, the persecution and intolerance perpetuated by those who claimed to be preaching Paul's message. By focusing only on Paul's mission to the Gentiles, by ignoring his Pharisaic background and his deep Jewish roots, the church cut itself off from the stock of Judaism even as it claimed to be true Israel. The resultant isolation of the Jews, the inquisitions, and the pogroms that followed this misrepresentation of Paul (and Jesus) are too sad and too well known to bear repetition. The litany of horrors perpetrated in the name of Christ's love and Paul's zeal is long and sorry. The shock of its most extreme perversion—the Nazi Holocaust—finally has brought Christianity up short. For the past half century there has been a great deal of soul-searching among Christian theologians. How could a message of love have brought Christians to such barbaric acts?

Along with that soul-searching there has been a concerted effort on the part of Christianity to uncover a clearer picture of Jesus and Paul. This attempt to return to the founders of Christianity must be applauded by Christians and Jews alike. While no Jew can accept Jesus Christ as Savior, every Jew must recognize the genius of the message of Jesus' gospel. Equally, every Jew recognizes that Paul is at heart a Pharisee. While his message may not be the same as that of (later) rabbinic Judaism—for no rabbinic Jew would suggest any distinction whatsoever between faith and works—the Pharisaic Jewish roots of Paul are clear. This refers not only to Paul's own claim of Pharisaic schooling but to much that is in the heart of his preaching and teaching. It behooves all of us, Christian and Jew alike, to recall that we spring from the same stock of biblical Israel. Paul, a student of Gamaliel, and Jesus, a Palestinian teacher whose students appropriately called him rabbi, both teach lessons of Torah.

This is not to say that Christianity and Judaism are the same. Nor is it to suggest at all that Jews must be receptive to Christianity. Nor—and this is essential to respecting the Jewish roots of Christianity's founders—nor does this suggest that Christianity in any way replaces or supersedes Judaism. But it does recognize that the two religions are sisters. Both share a worldview of history. Both share a Hebrew Bible as part of the central core of their respective canons. And both, at long last, are deeply in need of reconciliation with one another.

There are those in either camp that may not yet be ready for reconciling. Some will reject the notion that Christians and Jews share anything in common. There are those who will persist in seeing either their Judaism or their Christianity as superior to the other religion. They may have yet another millennium and more to wait for rapprochement. But for many Jews and Christians the time has come to walk together into the future.

Brad Young is one of the important theologians who is leading the way for Christians to explore the Jewish roots of Jesus, Paul, and Christianity. He is not a triumphalist. He is not interested in the conversion of the Jews. He believes and writes that Judaism has an essential place in God's scheme for salvation. He *is* interested in the conversion of Christianity, away from hatred and toward the love that Jesus preached. Brad Young has endeavored to excavate Paul's Pharisaic roots for all to examine, while at the same time leaving the family tree firmly planted and continuing to grow. Brad Young has been at the forefront of Jewish-Christian dialogue in this country.

As with Paul, one cannot help but be impressed with Brad Young and his force of personality. He sends forth brilliant students and makes clear his message. Some in the Christian and Jewish communities will disagree with him. But, many will see that it is Young's intention to reach out and remind both communities that we share much in common. Not everyone will have the blessing of meeting Brad Young. But, as with Paul, we do have his writings. He writes for both the Jewish and Christian communities to show them that while Christianity and Judaism differ profoundly on many issues, they spring from common ground. And, while Judaism and Christianity may differ, neither can be true to itself if it seeks to eradicate the other.

Brad Young has offered his vision of what Jesus and Paul had to teach. To offer this vision he has schooled himself in the details of Pharisaic Judaism, much as Paul—and before him, Jesus—did. And, like both of those towering figures of Christianity, Brad Young preaches a gospel that has a place of pride for Jews and Judaism. This does not diminish his Christianity. On the contrary, it defines and authenticates it. It is a Christianity that seems to this Pharisee, a twentieth-century rabbi, to be the message of the Christian Bible, a message of faith, hope, and charity.

1 Introduction

*Intensive research over many years has brought the writer of
the present book to a deep conviction that there is nothing in
the teaching of Paul—not even the most mystical elements
in it—that did not come to him from authentic Judaism.*

Joseph Klausner

THE New Testament describes the Apostle Paul as a Pharisee
who comes to faith in Jesus as the Messiah, boldly pro-
claiming the gospel as the power of the God of Israel unto
salvation, to the diverse peoples in distant parts of a Gentile
world. Working in a largely pagan environment, the one who
is referred to in the book of Acts as Saul of Tarsus establishes
churches as the Apostle Paul. Paul has been referred to as the
"second founder of Christianity." He has been called a "mys-
tic." Now he is referred to as a "Gnostic."[1] The consensus of
scholarship has come to view him as a Hellenistic Jew who
departed radically from his Judaism. Scholars view him as
being influenced by his upbringing in the Stoic environs of
Tarsus and various streams of thought flowing forth from
paganism, Greco-Roman culture, popular Hellenistic philosophy, mystery religious cults, and Gnostic systems. Seldom is
the origin of Paul's faith seen as rooted in Pharisaism.

This book begins with a different set of presuppositions.
Paul calls himself a Pharisee. We should listen to what Paul
tells us about himself. In fact, there is no evidence anywhere in
the New Testament that he departed from his firm convictions
as a Pharisee. Paul is a Jewish theologian who anchored his
beliefs in the Hebrew Bible and the teachings of his eminent

mentors in Jerusalem. He is a Hebrew of the Hebrews rather than a Hellenist of the Greeks. Fresh evidence from the literary discoveries of the Dead Sea Scrolls as well as renewed interest in the analysis of rabbinic literature place the Apostle Paul squarely within the Judaism of the land of Israel and not the Hellenism of Asia Minor, although surely there was much interaction between Hellenism and Judaism in the first century and this influenced Pharisaism.

Paul is a Pharisee who has been rejected by the synagogue and misunderstood by the church. The synagogue could not accept the profile of Paul's style of Pharisaism. For one thing, under the direction of the Sadducean high priests, he persecuted the early church. The leader of the Pharisees in those days, Rabban Gamaliel, fought hard against this type of religious persecution. For another thing, many Pharisees could not accept Paul's messianism based on his vision as he traveled the road to Damascus.[2] The early church, on the other hand, largely rejected the Jewish heritage of Paul by denying his Pharisaism. For the church, Paul is a former Pharisee. When he stopped persecuting the church, he departed from his Pharisaism. As a Pharisee, he was evil. As a Christian, he parted ways with his Judaic heritage to become a Christian.

Paul, however, considered himself to be a Pharisee throughout his entire life. He was proud of his Judaic heritage and his upbringing in Jerusalem. He studied the sources of his faith diligently. In many ways, Paul should qualify as a valuable source for the study of Pharisaism. He proclaimed himself to be a Pharisee in the line of Pharisees. He was dedicated to his faith and lived an observant life. In modern times, few people are as dedicated to their religious convictions as Paul. He practiced the life of Pharisaism in accordance with his family background and his training in the land of Israel.

By his belief in Jesus on the basis of his own dramatic encounter with the risen Messiah, Paul's religious fervor reached a higher plateau. For him, faith in Jesus as Messiah brought deeper conviction and enrichment. Above all, his energies were redirected toward the Gentile world. The Jewish apostle sought to call the pagan nations to a faith in the one God of Israel by preaching the message of Jesus the Messiah, "For, 'everyone who calls upon the name of the Lord will be saved' " (Rom 10:13).

By rejecting the Judaism of the Apostle Paul, unwittingly the church has adopted an anti-Semitism that echoes the teachings of Marcion, the second-century heretic who rejected the Old Testament for his interpretation of Paul's writings. Sometimes, as Christians, we have accepted Paul's teachings about Jesus while rejecting his love of the Hebrew Bible as well as his Judaic heritage. Abraham Joshua Heschel has noted the difficulty with this approach to Christian theology:

> The Christian message, which in its origins intended to be an affirmation and culmination of Judaism, became very early diverted into a repudiation and negation of Judaism; obsolescence and abrogation of Jewish faith became conviction and doctrine; the new covenant was conceived not as a new phase or disclosure but as abolition and replacement of the ancient one; theological thinking fashioned its terms in a spirit of antithesis to Judaism. Contrast and contradiction rather than acknowledgement of roots relatedness and indebtedness, became the perspective. Judaism a religion of law, Christianity a religion of grace; Judaism teaches a God of wrath, Christianity a God of love; Judaism a religion of slavish obedience, Christianity the conviction of free men; Judaism is particularism, Christianity is universalism; Judaism seeks work-righteousness, Christianity preaches faith-righteousness. The teaching of the old covenant a religion of fear, the gospel of the new covenant a religion of love . . .[3]

Today people long to understand Paul and his teachings. The time has come for a reevaluation of the foundation pillars of Paul's thought. His theology is rooted in Torah-true Judaism. His Pharisaism is evident in his teachings concerning the resurrection of the dead and in his interpretation of the Bible. He reveals knowledge of Jewish hermeneutics and halakah. When Paul is viewed as a Pharisee, many aspects of his teachings concerning grace and law are better understood. This is especially true when one realizes that the apostle was solving problems in congregations made up of both Jews and Gentiles.

Krister Stendahl has reminded us of the necessity for reading Paul's message in context:

> The main lines of Pauline interpretation—and hence both conscious and unconscious reading and quoting of Paul by scholars and lay people alike—have for many centuries been out of touch with one of the most basic of questions and concerns that shaped Paul's thinking in the first place: the relation between Jews and Gentiles.[4]

The context is the social and theological upheaval created among the early Christians when the pagan Gentiles began to enter the fellowship of believers. Paul approaches the situation from his Jewish heritage.

After all, Paul is a Pharisee living among the Christians, Jews, and pagan Gentiles. He is a bridge builder. He confronts hostilities from many factions in the church as well as from the Greco-Roman world in which he ministers. As a Jewish theologian, he labors diligently to win acceptance for non-Jews among all Christian believers, some of whom are most assuredly proselytes who converted to Judaism before they believed in Jesus. These ex-Gentile believers as well as many Pharisees in the early Jesus movement would demand total conversion, including circumcision for all Gentile converts. Paul the Pharisee argues against the requirement of circumcision for non-Jews coming to faith in the Messiah. Many would be offended by his gospel of grace. So Paul is a Pharisee among the Christians. It is his liberal attitude and free interpretation of the Torah that invites trouble for the apostle to the Gentiles.

Gaining awareness and insight into Paul's Jewish background promises to open new horizons for interpreting the message of this most controversial figure in nascent Christianity.

INTRODUCTION: NOTES

1. See E. P. Sanders, *Paul and Palestinian Judaism* (Philadelphia: Fortress, 1977); and P. Tomson, *Paul and the Jewish Law* (Philadelphia: Fortress, 1990). Tomson points out (p. 1) that regarding Paul, scholars routinely begin with three assumptions: "(1) the centre of his thought is a polemic against the Law; (2) the Law for him no longer had a practical meaning; and (3) ancient Jewish literature is no source for explaining his letters." All three of these presuppositions are wrong. Paul's Jewish theology is seldom appreciated. Cf. also the stimulating work and creative thought of Krister Stendahl, *Paul Among Jews and Gentiles* (Philadelphia: Fortress, 1976).

2. See the record of the New Testament: Acts 9:1–9, 26:12–23; Gal 1:12. Cf. the discussion of F. J. Foakes Jackson and Kirsopp Lake, *The Beginnings of Christianity* (5 vols.; Grand Rapids: Baker Book House, 1979) 4.99–102; F. F. Bruce, *The Acts of the Apostles* (Grand Rapids: Eerdmans, 1984) 196–200; and Otto Bauernfeind, *Kommentar und Studien zur Apostelgeschichte* (Tübingen: J.C.B. Mohr, 1980) 129–35.

3. Abraham Joshua Heschel, *The Insecurity of Freedom* (New York: Schocken, 1972) 169.

4. Stendahl, *Paul Among Jews and Gentiles*, 1.

Paul the Jewish Theologian

Let us plunge straight in and begin with Paul's origins.
It must be stressed quite emphatically, against a current
trend in scholarship which seeks to see Paul exclusively as a
"Hellenistic Diaspora Jew," that in his own testimonies, in the
letters, the Pharisee connected with Jewish Palestine stands
in the foreground, to whom Jerusalem seems to be more
important than anywhere else. Only from Luke do we learn
that he came from Tarsus, the capital of Cilicia, and that
he was a citizen of both Tarsus and Rome. Paul the author
of the letters no longer thinks this part of his past worth
mentioning; it seems to him to be much more remote than
his time as a Pharisee in Palestine.

Martin Hengel

PAUL was Jewish. He was a theologian. But is it possible to describe Paul as a Jewish theologian? Sometimes Paul's rich Hebrew heritage has been hidden from view because of his work among the Gentiles. After all, first and foremost Paul is remembered as a Jewish apostle to the Gentiles. Such a career is doomed to stir up debate. Paul's life has never disappointed the journalist breed of individual who is looking for some kind of religious or political ruckus. As a pioneer theologian, Paul created problems for his own people—the Jews—as well as for the Gentiles. Going beyond his own culture and faith, Paul crossed over into diverse cultural settings and interfaith relationships. Yet he still referred to himself as a Pharisee.

Paul stepped outside his own Jewish environment to assume a leading role in an international outreach to the multiethnic peoples of Asia Minor. He was sent to the Gentile nations. So perhaps the first question that we should ask relates to Paul's own background: Was Paul influenced more by Tarsus or Jerusalem? While he was born in Tarsus, Paul lived and studied in Jerusalem.[1] Was he authentically Jewish in his approach to his religious teachings and efforts to bear witness to his experience? Later in life, Paul worked primarily among the Gentiles. Indeed, he challenged the dominant religious views of his time, preaching against the syncretistic religious pluralism and various forms of idolatry he encountered everywhere he went.[2] Through the coming of the Jewish Messiah he saw the righteousness of God revealed to those who were far away. Clearly Paul's work among the Gentiles and our unfamiliarity with ancient Judaism make understanding his Jewish theology difficult. In spite of this, his mission to the Gentiles is deeply rooted in his Jewish way of thinking. His upbringing as a Pharisee molded his character and guided his teachings. His writings, moreover, have both captured the hearts of many disciples and enraged numerous antagonists.[3] As a religious genius who built bridges between diverse communities and as a letter writer who treated complex issues of faith and practice, Paul has always excited lively debate within his circle of followers as well as among his adversaries. Often we misunderstand Paul: first, because we do not know the problems he was trying to solve, and second, perhaps even more significantly, because we do not know very much about his Jewish faith and culture. The Judaism of Paul must be the starting point for any serious analysis of his writings.

Reading the epistles of Paul with comprehension, consequently, presents quite a challenging undertaking. After all, reading someone else's mail tends to be confusing and oftentimes reveals some unexpected surprises. Studying the Pauline epistles has been compared to the popular television game show *Jeopardy!*. To play this game, contestants are given an answer to a hidden question. Then they must guess what the question is, based upon what they can learn from the answer. The audience delights in watching the contestants struggling with the answers, trying to identify the questions. It is much more entertaining than simply asking the contestants questions that they are expected to answer. By way of comparison, studying Paul's correspondence is like reading answers without the questions. The student of Paul's writings is forced to guess what the original questions surrounding his correspondence really were.

In a similar way, eavesdropping on one side of a phone conversation can be a very perplexing enterprise. One cannot always be sure of the topic under discussion. In the Epistles, one line is open, and modern-day readers are eavesdropping. Paul answers questions for his friends and treats serious matters of faith and practice for the congregations with whom he corresponds. The other line, however, is not connected.[4] Today no one knows what was the exact nature of the diverse problems confronting the original readers of Paul's epistles. That line is closed.

Nonetheless, one thing is certain. The Jewish apostle to the Gentiles is well known for the controversy he stirred up wherever he traveled. Times were changing in the Roman Empire, and Paul was a major figure in the blossoming movement of Jesus' followers, which was spreading beyond the borders of the land of Israel. Paul's teachings flow from what David Flusser has called the second stratum of Christianity.[5] The first stratum was laid in the life of Jesus and in the movement of his earlier followers, who were active before Pauline thought became so influential. Jesus labored among his own people on the soil of the land of Israel, whereas Paul crossed the border, breaking down walls of separation between Christians, Jews, and Gentiles. But surely the message of Paul would be better appreciated if the questions he treated were more accessible to later readers. No doubt the apostle invited dialogue with his correspondence and sometimes desired an interactive response. The reader of Paul's congregational correspondence must remember that these epistles are open letters. Each reader must try to decipher the message and understand its significance within Paul's original context.

What makes Paul so difficult to understand? Why do scholars and ordinary readers of the apostle's letters come up with such different answers to questions concerning Paul's life and teachings? First, as has been mentioned already, a number of key issues can be resolved only by correctly identifying those questions Paul was answering. But the major difficulty in grasping Paul's thought is really context. We misunderstand Paul because we do not understand his Jewish faith. Without esteeming Paul's Judaism, we cannot comprehend his message. Striving to identify the questions Paul was answering is a first step. But the serious reader of Paul's letters must struggle with the thinking of a Pharisee who studied in Jerusalem. A more intimate knowledge of Paul's Judaism unlocks the mysteries of his religious experience. So the Judaism of Jerusalem, rather than the paganism of Tarsus, seems to be the foundation for Paul's approach to the problems besetting the early Christian congregations to whom he directed his correspondence.

Much of the controversy ultimately stems from questions concerning Paul's own background. Was Paul a hellenized Greek Jew from Tarsus? Or was he a Pharisee trained by Gamaliel in Jerusalem? Did he cancel the Torah once and for all? Have works of Torah lost significance because of faith? Did he exclude the Jewish people from the family of God by speaking of the church as the new Israel that completely replaced the old? Did he deny the teachings of Jesus and become the second founder of Christianity? What is crucial for Pauline theology? What would be his "ultimate concern"—to use the overly burdened terminology of yet another famous theologian named Paul but with the family name of Tillich?

The Apostle Paul did not belong to the circles of systematic theologians from Germany or any other Western nation. This Paul's theology was rooted in Judaism from late antiquity, and his family heritage was Jewish stock. He was from the Middle East. His mentality was quite different from that of the West. How, then, can the modern reader of Paul, whether he or she ascribes to the apostle's doctrine or admittedly feels uncomfortable with some of his ideas, make peace with the enthusiastic Jewish preacher to the Gentiles?

To make peace with Paul, we must listen carefully to the apostle's message in his original cultural context. The starting point is crucial. When the starting point is Paul's Jewish theology, many issues of his cultural environment are resolved. To study Paul, we must begin somewhere. Where we begin, moreover, determines the course of research and the impact of the final conclusions. Most scholars begin in Tarsus. Here, however, I will contend that Paul's theology is more a product of Jerusalem than of Tarsus. Paul never canceled Torah, but made the necessary distinctives between Jews and Gentiles in the mysterious plan of God. He taught that the Gentiles were grafted into the olive tree Israel, and he never intended for a replacement theology to take root in the Christian church. In dealing with matters of concern among the Christian communities, Paul upheld the teachings of Jesus as well as the authority of the law and the prophets. Ultimately, Paul discovered self-fulfillment and personal pride in his mission of leading the pagan Gentiles into the family of God by faith in Jesus the Messiah. The resurrection power of Jesus flowed through his life in a deep spiritual experience in which Paul felt the presence of God. At least in Paul's view, the Holy Spirit empowered him to live a life pleasing to God. By dying to himself and experiencing the Messiah's resurrection through faith, the apostle could obey God. All the while, he was filled with expectancy as he looked ahead to the final redemption that would appear in the future when all Israel would be saved.

The contours of Paul's thought must be sought in his cultural setting. Jerusalem is the starting point. The Apostle Paul, moreover, is a conceptual theologian. He makes use of interactive theological concepts. Paul's theology begins with an unshakable faith in the one God of Israel. Paul possesses a great love, derived from his rich Hebrew heritage, for all humanity. Indeed, Paul himself tells his followers that, concerning the law, he is a Pharisee.

Like other Pharisees, Paul believed in reward and punishment from God. Every human being will experience either God's abundant grace or divine wrath in the day of retribution. When dealing with the towering issues of his day, he affirmed the validity of Torah in his teachings and practical theology. Because of his belief in the goodness of God, Paul, like other Pharisees, had looked for a future redeemer who would resemble Moses and bring help to people in need. Paul's approach to the Bible is paralleled in similar interpretations among the sages of ancient Israel as well as in the precious manuscripts of the Dead Sea Scrolls. But in contrast, Paul focused upon Jesus as the anointed one designated to bring God's goodness to all humanity, including the pagan Gentiles. He struggled with the seeming contradiction of a suffering Messiah and a future redeemer. After the experience with Jesus on the road to Damascus, Paul was driven by a renewed, heightened awareness of the divine presence and a consuming desire to bear witness to the pagan cultures of the world. In any event, as can be seen in his writings, Paul quoted the Bible frequently and discussed its application among Jews and Gentiles. Indeed, he talked about Torah constantly. His incessant occupation with the biblical foundation of his beliefs and his conceptual approach to his interactive theology might even be described as a passion. Why would Paul talk about Torah so much? Because he was a Jewish theologian. He was a Pharisee who sought the wisdom of Torah for guidance and direction.

TARSUS OR JERUSALEM?

What was Paul really like? Many have tried to describe him, and probably every reader of his epistles creates his or her own mental picture of the fiery Jew from Jerusalem. Though he was born in Tarsus, he grew up in Jerusalem. His parents may have brought the young Paul to Jerusalem solely for the purpose of Jewish education. Many residing in the Jewish communities outside the land of Israel went up· to Jerusalem in order to study and learn. It is likely that Paul's father brought Paul, a Pharisee among Pharisees, to the national homeland for the sake of Torah learning. Paul studied under the grandson of Hillel, Gamaliel the Elder, and possessed an overriding zeal for his faith. Hillel himself came to Jerusalem from the Jewish Diaspora in Babylon. Hillel is sometimes referred to as "the Babylonian," especially in the Babylonian Talmud. It should not be surprising, then, that Acts refers to Paul as "Saul of Tarsus." The move from Tarsus to Jerusalem, nonetheless, most likely occurred very early in Paul's childhood. Paul himself never mentions Tarsus in his letters.

While we learn something about Paul's background and upbringing from the New Testament, it does not reveal the way Paul looked. Probably the earliest physical description of Paul is found in the apocryphal *Acts of Paul:*

> A man of little stature, thin-haired upon the head, crooked in the legs, of good state of body, with eyebrows joining, and nose somewhat hooked, full of grace: for sometimes he appeared like a man, and sometimes he had the face of an angel.[6]

Paul's mother would not have been too pleased with this description of her son's physical features, but she may well have sensed the boy's strong-willed personality at a tender age. He was short, balding, and bowlegged, and his bushy eyebrows joining together remind one of a modern-day villain. But the inward force of Paul's personality is emphasized in this apocryphal depiction.

At Lystra, during Paul's first missionary journey, the people assumed Paul to be the Greek god Hermes. Was this because of his eloquent speech or his clean appearance? Paul displayed humility about his eloquence. Perhaps his appearance reminded the people of the many artistic expressions of Hermes in the popular religious cults of the area. Barnabas, Paul's distinguished traveling companion, was taken for Zeus. No doubt it was Barnabas' older and more mature dignity that invited such an association between him and Zeus. The book of Acts records that when Paul came to Lystra, he observed a crippled man who possessed faith. He looked at him and said, "Stand upright on your feet" (Acts 14:10). Seeing that the man had been healed, the people of the city rushed over to Paul and Barnabas. They wanted to deify the pair and offer sacrifice to them as gods. Imagine the shock! Paul was a Pharisee. From his earliest days he had been inculcated with the reality that there was only one true living God.

In any case, much more can be learned about Paul's background as a Pharisee than can be known about his appearance, which is merely speculation. But probably most students of the New Testament already have developed firm ideas concerning the controversial apostle. Some view him as a traitor. Still others see him in a positive light as a great teacher or an evangelist. For many he is a model missionary. In popular discussions, he assumes various roles and takes on quite strong characteristics. He lived life boldly and has become as much a legend as he was a historical figure.

Two types of evidence will be considered here to describe Paul. One source is the record of the book of Acts. The other is what he tells his readers about himself in his epistles—this is of primary importance. Many of his readers knew him personally. Therefore, he could not speak about himself in wildly exaggerated terms. At any rate, one discovers many differences between modern popular descriptions of Paul and what the apostle actually tells us about himself. In the case of Paul, the many inconsistencies between Tarsus and Jerusalem are decisive.

It is from the book of Acts that we learn that Paul was born in Tarsus (Acts 9:11). And only through the record of the book of Acts is Paul's Roman citizenship revealed (Acts 22:25).[7] On his final trip to Jerusalem, Paul was arrested in the temple and carried away by Roman soldiers. When he was being arrested on the Temple Mount, Paul fearlessly made a request to the Roman cohort. The military commander apparently noticed Paul's accent. He asked the apostle, "Do you know Greek?" He appeared surprised that Paul addressed him in the Greek language. Paul wrote Greek as if it were his mother language. Even if his style would not be described as eloquent by a classicist, he possessed an extensive knowledge of Greek. And when the Roman soldier heard Paul's question, he detected the accent of a foreigner speaking Greek.

A notorious messianic pretender, known as the Egyptian, was wanted by the Roman authorities. The Egyptian had led a sizable group of his followers into the desert, where he promised to bring redemption to his people in the same way another Egyptian, Moses, had led the people of Israel into the desert for their deliverance. The Romans captured and slaughtered many of this notorious false messiah's followers, but the so-called Egyptian himself escaped. When the Roman commander was quick to accuse Paul of being the Egyptian, Paul denied the charge. It was a case of mistaken identity. Paul explained to the Roman military man, "I am a Jew, from Tarsus in Cilicia, a citizen of no mean city" (Acts 21:39).

Indeed, Tarsus was no mean city. Connected to the Mediterranean Sea by the Cydnus River, it was strategically located, a thriving center of commerce, Greek culture, and philosophic learning. The city had a university and was greatly influenced by the Stoic philosophical schools. It was the birthplace of

Chrysippus, the well-known leader of the Stoic movement in the third century BC. Many scholars have detected an element of Stoic philosophy in Paul when he wrote, "Not that I complain of want; for I have learned, in whatever state I am, to be content. . . . I can do all through Christ who strengthens me" (Phil 4:11–13). A Stoic philosopher could accept hardship with serenity and a sound mind, though the Stoic would not look for inner strength from Jesus. Certainly Paul's birthplace had its impact upon the apostle. The ancient geographer Strabo praised the keen educational interest of its citizens:

> The people at Tarsus have devoted themselves so eagerly, not only to philosophy, but also to the whole round of education in general, that they have surpassed Athens, Alexandria or any other place that can be named where there have been schools and lectures of philosophers.[8]

The Roman cohort who had arrested Paul apparently was so impressed with Paul's courage, background, and knowledge of Greek that he allowed him to address the crowds in the temple that day. The shock, however, is that Paul spoke to the crowd in Hebrew, not in Greek or Aramaic. On the one hand, the Roman soldier seemed surprised that Paul could speak Greek so well; on the other, the people whom he addressed on the Temple Mount seemed impressed that he could speak to them in the Hebrew language. In this scene from the Acts of the Apostles, the connection between Tarsus and Jerusalem is illuminated. In some ways Paul was at home in both cultures. The content of his speech definitively demonstrates that he was bilingual, fluent in both Greek and Hebrew. Paul clearly told the people that although he was born in Tarsus of Cilicia, he had been raised in Jerusalem. Moreover, he studied at the feet of Gamaliel. The phrase "at the feet of" is a technical expression found in Jewish literature to indicate serious discipleship.

Paul also revealed on this occasion that he was "educated according to the strict manner of the law of our fathers," which most probably was a reference to the spiritual heritage of the Pharisees. But unlike most other Pharisees, and especially his reputed teacher Gamaliel, who protected leaders of the Jesus movement such as Peter and the apostles, Paul had collaborated with the Sadducees.[9] In his zeal for God, he had once felt that it was his duty to persecute the early church. Paul's sincere "no" to Jesus and his followers was his "yes" to God, although it seemed greatly misguided in the eyes of the Christians. All this changed when he had an experience on the way to Damascus. Ironically, Paul's personal encounter with the risen Lord occurred as he was carrying letters, written by the high priest himself, sanctioning the arrest of believers in Damascus. The high priest was a Sadducee, and the Sadducees were closely linked to the Roman authorities. Paul's motivation for persecuting the Christians was fueled by the politics of the Sadducees and the Romans rather than by the religious piety of the Pharisees.

A PHARISEE AMONG THE CHRISTIANS

Paul's background in the book of Acts is very informative for a careful reading of his epistles. In contrast to popular depictions of the apostle in modern times, Paul in his epistles gives a quite distinct portrayal of himself. He does not describe himself as a Hellenistic Jew or a Gnostic believer. According to Paul, he was born of the people of Israel and circumcised on the eighth day. In his family tradition, he knew that he came from the tribe of Benjamin. Paul describes himself as a Hebrew of the Hebrews, which probably reflects a cultural disposition as well as linguistic ability. It may well indicate that Hebrew was his mother tongue or the language spoken in his home. He is a Pharisee in his religious orientation. Paul is even bold enough to say that he is blameless before the law. Such a remark only reflects his strong commitment to orthodox religious observance. Paul was not without sin, but he could be forgiven, like all members of the Jewish community. After all, according to the teachings of the Pharisees, God's great compassion is revealed when people ask for forgiveness. No one could live a life without sin, but each individual could be blameless before God as he or she asked for forgiveness and lived an observant life. Paul celebrated the Jewish festivals.

The apostle does not refer to himself as a Stoic philosopher. It is perhaps worthwhile to observe what he does *not* say about himself. Paul does not claim to be a Greek of the Greeks or even a Jew who is conversant in Greek language and culture. He does not emphasize any training he received in philosophy. According to the two best sources for his life—the book of Acts and his own writings—Paul is a Pharisee. The scholar should pursue every discipline of research that may shed light on Pauline thought, including Stoic philosophy, Epicureanism, Greek mystery religions, Gnostic religious systems, Hermetic writings, and the rich imagination of the religious minds who created such masterpieces as have recently been discovered in the Nag Hammadi codices—all fascinating currents of comparative study. Spheres of influence outside the parameters of ancient Judaism or those only indirectly touched by Jewish thought should never be ignored. Nevertheless, even though all of these studies may provide insight into Paul's thought and his work among the pagan nations, the apostle's own self-portrait is of foremost importance. Paul describes himself as a Pharisee.

The Jewish roots of his "ultimate concern" are sometimes neglected. Yet the value of the Jewish background to Paul's teachings cannot be overemphasized. Indeed, the religious literature of the treasured Dead Sea Scrolls demonstrates remarkable parallels between Paul and the authors of these Hebrew manuscripts. Paul is a Hebrew of the Hebrews. Paul was much more in his element when he sat at the feet of Gamaliel in the academies of learning in Jerusalem than when he was placed in the halls of the philosophic schools of thought influenced by Chrysippus in Tarsus.

PAUL AND JERUSALEM

Paul was from Jerusalem. In Acts, he says that he grew up in Jerusalem. His relatives were living in the holy city. The son of Paul's sister was residing in Jerusalem when Paul was held in custody in the Roman prison, which was probably located in the fortress of Antonia (Acts 23:16). His nephew caught wind of a murder plot: the plotters planned to ambush Paul during a prisoner transfer. How did the nephew find out? The family of Paul seems to have had some influence in the city and been acquainted with the local gossip. At any rate, Acts suggests that Paul and his family were not at all strangers to the holy city. During his confinement, Paul's nephew was able to visit him and explain the scheme to kill him. When Paul asked the Roman guard to take the young man to the Roman cohort, the centurion obeyed.

Paul's connection to Jerusalem ran deep into the political organization, the social structure, the religious institutions, and the centers of learning in the city. Paul knew the operation of his place of confinement. His family had connections in the city. Earlier, Paul had been authorized to persecute Christians in Damascus. He had studied at the feet of Gamaliel. Furthermore, he knew enough about the differences between the Pharisees and the Sadducees to use their strong theological disagreements among themselves for his own advantage in the judicial proceedings against him (Acts 23:6–10). When he was led before the council, he realized that some were Pharisees and others were Sadducees. So Paul mentioned the resurrection, and a great clamor of debate arose between the factions of the Sadducees and the Pharisees.

The members of the council were more interested in debating the theological issue of the resurrection than in dealing with Paul's case. Paul was at home in the tense atmosphere of religious debate. He was familiar with the inner workings of the different factions in Jerusalem, and he knew that his friends among the Pharisees would support him. He was not disappointed. The Pharisees argued on Paul's behalf; they stood up and contended, "We find nothing wrong in this man" (Acts 23:9).[10] After all, Paul had already declared, "I am a Pharisee." This declaration, moreover, was made many years after his Damascus Road experience.

PAUL AND TORAH

Paul's Jerusalem connection is essential for a proper understanding of his theological writings. One feature of Paul's correspondence is unmistakable—his extensive use of the Bible. For him all authority is derived from the teachings of Torah. In Torah he unravels the promise of the coming Messiah, whom he has discovered through his personal experience to be Jesus. But the teachings of the Bible are more to Paul than proofs for the messianic mission of Jesus.[11] The Torah, Prophets, and Writings are not merely a reservoir of proof texts from which Paul draws to inculcate would-be converts. On the contrary, Paul employs the Bible as his primary source of faith and practice.

The Hebrew Scriptures are the foundation of his teachings. In Gal 5:3 he writes, "I testify again to every man who receives circumcision that he is bound to keep the whole law."[12] Was Paul circumcised? Did he ever stop obeying the teachings of Torah? This verse from Galatians must be recognized for its far-reaching implications. It suggests that Paul continued to live an observant life even after his experience on the road to Damascus. Though he became all things to all people so that he might win them for the Lord (1 Cor

9:19–23), this does not mean that he stopped living an observant life. He would not rob a bank to win a bank robber or commit murder to convince a murderer. Paul was a man of integrity.

Like other Pharisees and religious Jews, the Apostle Paul would deal with issues of ritual practice in each situation according to his understanding of Torah. Other Pharisees had relationships with non-Jews and traveled in areas that restricted their freedom of ritual observance. Religious Jews were required to know Torah and its accepted interpretations in order to properly adjust their ritual observance in different circumstances. As a Pharisee, eating pork would be a very troublesome proposition for Paul; he would probably much prefer a vegetarian menu as an alternative. Upholding the commandment of love, however, was pivotal in the apostle's relationships with others. Indeed, Paul never denies the validity of Torah as revealing God's will. Even in Galatians, he affirms that the whole law is fulfilled in the commandment "Love thy neighbor as thyself" (Lev 19:18).[13] By strictly observing the principle of love, a person is able to fulfill all the requirements of Torah regarding interpersonal relationships.

Paul did not want the non-Jew believing in Jesus to be circumcised and take on the ceremonial observance of all the laws of Torah. But would he seek to remove the marks of circumcision in his own body and deny the essence of the covenant God made with the Jewish people? The apostle was proud of his heritage, which attained deeper meaning for him in the coming of Jesus. His job was teaching Gentiles about the Lord and winning acceptance for them in a community of faith where many thought that circumcision and total observance of Torah should be a required of each individual believer: both Jews and proselytes esteemed the covenant of circumcision. The proselytes who believed in Jesus were the strongest opponents of Paul's gospel of grace, which allowed Gentiles to enter the community without circumcision. Alan

Segal notes the irony of the situation: "Paul's preaching would have offended the circumcised, ex-gentile Christian." After all, the ex-Gentile believers had become proselytes to Judaism first. They had already been circumcised and had accepted the difficult challenge of living everyday life as religious Jews. Should other Gentiles be accepted in any other way? "Paul took the role of representative of Gentile Christianity seriously. Thus we have a double irony. Circumcision was defended by gentiles who had undergone circumcision to become Jews, and the gospel of the uncircumcised was defended by a former Pharisee."[14]

Perhaps some Pharisees would have rejected him, but Paul does not seem to reject Pharisaism. Even his doctrine of the coming of the Messiah is rooted in Pharisaic teachings, though many of Paul's Pharisee colleagues would take issue with his final analysis. In any event, Paul, the Pharisee among the Christians, was trying to build a bridge between the diverse groups flowing into the popular Jesus movement. He was spearheading the missionary outreach to the pagan Gentiles. As a Pharisee, born in Tarsus but educated in Jerusalem, he was able to reach out to the different factions, seeking reconciliation between them. Paul argued vigorously his very strong opinions concerning this issue.

Paul did not cancel the law. In Galatians he is not opposed to the observance of Torah. On the contrary, he upholds the teachings of Torah. But in Jewish theology the teachings of Torah have a different application for Jews, who are from the circumcision and thus part of the covenant relationship, than they have for non-Jews, who have not entered fully into God's covenant with the people of Israel. Can they, too, be included?

Paul's answers to questions concerning the life of the Christian communities were rooted in Torah interpretation and underscore his background as a Pharisee. He possessed a bubbly personality. The words of the Bible flowed through his thought patterns as if they came straight from his heart. In

accordance with Jewish practice, Paul must have memorized
much Scripture and oral tradition. Gnostics might be interested in the Bible to understand the creation of the world.
Greek philosophers sought wisdom where it might be found,
even in the Bible. But Paul studied Torah for a different
reason. First, he affirmed the validity of Torah for illuminating
the significance of the coming of Jesus. But he did not begin
there, because he was a Pharisee with a strong education in the
Bible in his pre-Christian days. Paul did not stop there, because as a Pharisee, Paul viewed Torah as giving divine revelation for holy living. Paul learned the teachings of Torah in
order to understand the mystery of God and to revere him by
entering into a life of obedience. The apostle loved the Hebrew
Scriptures and lived his life in accordance with the moral and
spiritual values expressed in them.

LAW OR TORAH?

Paul's view of Torah and his whole cultural orientation
evolved during the years he trained in Jerusalem under the
guidance of Gamaliel, and presumably other Pharisaic leaders
as well. His approach to the Bible and the system of interpretation he used to expound it was basically that of the Pharisees.
While scholars have struggled with the possible meanings of
the law in Paul's theology, a Jewish view of Torah closely
associated with rabbinic-Pharisaic thinking provides the most
productive model. Why must there exist different meanings
for the Greek term *nomos* in Paul's letters? When Paul used
nomos, he was referring to Torah within the context of Judaism. Paul does not mean natural law, as distinct from spiritual
law, or the various other suggestions for the meaning of *nomos*. The Hebrew concept of Torah is Paul's intended meaning.
Law is a poor translation of *nomos* in Paul's writings. This
translation stems from the Latin Vulgate. In it *nomos* is translated by the Latin word *lex,* which means "law." For Paul

nomos has a vastly greater significance than the concept of law. Although in his letters Paul quotes the Bible according to the Septuagint as the accepted translation for his Greek-speaking congregations, his theology is thoroughly Hebraic. He is thinking Torah, not law.

When the translation of *nomos* as "law" becomes normative in English discussions of Pauline thought, a great deal of the apostle's Hebrew heritage is eradicated from his life experience. He could only see the world through his understanding of Torah. For a Pharisee such as Paul, Torah was an all-consuming passion. It was the apostle's cherished tradition. It guided his way of living from day to day. Torah for Paul, as it was for Israel's sages, is as vast as God himself. Torah teaches God's higher purposes and reaches far beyond a simple enumeration of the five books of Moses.

Torah is spiritual. When Paul writes, "The law of the Spirit of life," in Rom 8:2, he is referring to the higher meaning of Torah. It is a spiritual force. The same Torah that gives life through Jesus the Messiah, in Paul's thought, also exposes human need and moral failure. Torah is both the "law of the Spirit" and the "law of sin and death" (Rom 8:2). All depends upon the human response to the divine initiative. In Paul's thinking, Torah is good. The apostle declares, "So the law is holy, and the commandment is holy and just and good" (Rom 7:12). The problem is human weakness. In his weakness Paul had failed to live by the higher principle of God's reign, and in this respect Torah had shown his own shortcoming. Only because of human weakness can Torah be spoken of within the framework of sin and death. But because of God's mercy, it is spirit and life. Hence, Torah means both the "law of the Spirit" and the "law of sin and death." Through his experience with the power of the Holy Spirit, Paul reached beyond to the greater force of Torah in his personal encounter with daily living. Holding Torah in high esteem, he applied it in every aspect of life. Paul revealed an intense passion for the higher meaning of Torah.

The anti-Judaism of the church has roots running deep into the core of her history. The early-second-century heretic Marcion completely rejected the Hebrew Bible. Although many church leaders fought his doctrines, at times Marcion's theology managed to infiltrate orthodox teachings.[15] As Christians, we have learned about Judaism from one-sided accounts of inner struggles within the church and have viewed Jews and Judaism from our own biased perspective. We receive a derivative view of Judaism based upon false evidence. Without having read the ancient literature Israel's sages left behind, we malign Judaism as a religious system of legalism with a salvation-by-works infrastructure.[16] The heresy of Marcion's teachings tainted unfavorably the progression of ecclesiastical doctrines. Christianity became defined as the antithesis of the faith experience of the Jewish people. The acknowledgment of roots relatedness and interconnectedness between the mother—Judaism—and her daughter faith was obscured by a battle of hate and polemic. Paul's experience, nevertheless, was vastly different. He experienced Torah learning at the feet of Israel's most notable sages. Perhaps the time has finally come for us as Christians to learn about Judaism firsthand from the rich sources of Jewish belief rather than from the prejudices of the past. We can study the sayings attributed to Gamaliel in the talmudic literature for our own enrichment and understanding of God's nature and, of course, for better comprehension of Paul.

PAUL'S CONCEPTUAL APPROACH

In Paul's day, the essence of Jewish faith had little to do with an earn-your-salvation religious system. Jewish faith begins with the nature of God. He is one. He is compassionate and full of grace. In Exod 34:6, this high, lofty Hebrew idea of God is expressed: "The LORD, the LORD God, merciful and gracious, long-suffering and abundant in goodness and truth."

The Hebrew mind viewed God quite differently from the systematic theological thinking of the West, which defines God and his work with creation in a linear manner. The Western-style treatment of the divine character attempts to explain inconsistencies and harmonize contradictions systematically. The Hebrew mind was filled with wonder at the mystery of God. The vastness of God and his inscrutable ways left them awestruck. Inconsistencies and contradictions are intimately related to human, finite understandings of the infinite God. He is beyond human comprehension. First-century Jews approached God through an interactive associative mentality. The fact that God is incomprehensible is very much a part of Jewish thought processes. The Western mind, however, explains everything but understands so little of the divine nature. The Hebrew mind, on the other hand, is overpowered by a sense of wonder and amazement.[17] It thrives on the inconsistencies and contradictions of the one awe-inspiring God.

Paul has a conceptual approach to theology. It is not linear. His theological worldview is circular and interactive. A systematic approach to Paul draws a straight line and follows his reasoning from creation and the fall all the way along to the redemptive suffering of Jesus and the second coming. But Paul is much more complex and far less linear and systematic. On the one hand, Paul views history as moving toward the goal of God's final redemptive plan, which will culminate in the Parousia and the eschatological judgment; on the other, he views God through the prism of perplexing curiosity, which inspires wonder. He does not preach a cycle of salvation history, but the apostle does conceive of the divine ways in a circular dynamic process. In his contemplation of the mystery of God, like other Jewish theologians of his day, the apostle is content to leave questions unanswered and inconsistencies unresolved. He views theology as a conceptual whole.

Torah encompasses so much of what can be known about God in the conceptual worldview. Max Kadushin has tried to describe rabbinic theology in these terms.[18] As will be seen, this approach is quite effective for Paul's view of Torah. Paul focuses on the sum of the whole instead of dissecting the individual parts. As Kadushin points out, the rabbis could not speak about the kingdom of heaven without a myriad of verses coming into their minds. Not only did they realize that these Bible passages possess a literal meaning, but they pushed beyond to deeper realms of Torah learning. It is a conceptual approach. The mere mention of the term "kingdom of heaven" brought to their minds verses such as "The LORD reigns forever and ever" (Exod 15:18) and "The LORD reigns" (Ps 93:1). Although these passages mention only that the Lord reigns, for the rabbis they refer to the kingdom of heaven. Through the conceptual approach of the rabbinic mind, many other meanings were associated with God's reign. The kingdom conveys a cluster of theological ideas. In the higher view of Torah, God's reign means affirming who God is by praying, "Hear O Israel, the LORD our God, the LORD is one." The kingdom of heaven means obedience to the command-ments. It refers to the deliverance of the people from the yoke of bondage in Egypt and their great liberty when they entered the promised land. It is divine protection and God's salvation. In Jewish thought, one discovers a rich associative method. The theological ideas come in clusters. So it is with Paul. His theology is not systematic; rather, it comprises clusters of associated concepts. Describing the vitality of Paul's flowing discussions, Hans J. Schoeps has revealed the apostle's vibrant persona:

> Paul was a dynamic personality, on whom thoughts rained so that he was driven ceaselessly from one to the other. Moreover, his thought was penetrating, leading us to well-nigh unfathomable depths. Often he merely suggests and instead of a whole chain of thought will give us flashes of ideas.[19]

Torah for Paul cannot be defined simply by the term *law* in English. The term *Torah* expresses the highest dimension of

Jewish experience because it reveals the nature of God to his people. Torah encompasses all that is known about God and his love for each individual created in the divine image. Paul possesses a passion for Torah as the quintessential self-disclosure of God and the divine will. Its preeminent purpose is found in Jesus the Messiah because, as Paul declares, now the Gentiles have been grafted into the olive tree (Rom 10:4). He glories in his ministry as the Jewish apostle to the pagan nations. For Paul, Torah has not lost its force after the coming of Jesus, but now Jews and Gentiles occupy their distinctive positions in the mystery of God's higher plan.

As a Pharisee, the focal point of Paul's thought was Torah. After his experience on the road to Damascus, Torah for Paul took on a deeper meaning in the coming of Jesus. Paul's Torah-centered theology was eclipsed with an understanding of the Messiah as the higher purpose of Torah. The great vision of the Hebrew prophets is realized when the Gentiles come into a relationship with the one God of Israel.[20]

REPLACEMENT OR ENGRAFTMENT?

Has God rejected his people? The mere idea of God's rejection of his people was repugnant to Paul. The apostle declares, "The gifts and call of God are irrevocable" (Rom 11:29). In Paul's mind, God does not break his promise to Israel in order to reach out to the Gentiles. Paul prefers to speak of a great mystery. Instead of explaining everything like a brilliant theologian, Paul is awestruck at the mystery of God. In the passion of a Hebrew prophet, he is filled with wonder and amazement.

Paul makes one thing clear for his Gentile readers concerning the people of Israel, for whose sake Paul would wish that he himself could be cut off from Jesus.[21] The depth of Paul's emotion is overwhelming. Despite the fact that the Jewish people as a whole have not come, like himself, to a faith in Jesus, he possesses an all-consuming and unconditional love for his own. The apostle is referring to the Israelites according to the flesh who have not come to believe in Jesus. The one major point for him is that God has not rejected the people of Israel. Paul begins his discussion of the great mystery of God's higher purposes by affirming the irrevocable divine call that was made to the Jewish people.

> They are Israelites, and to them belong the sonship, the glory, the covenants, the giving of the law, the worship, and the promises; to them belong the patriarchs, and of their race, according to the flesh is the Christ. God who is over all be blessed for ever. Amen. (Rom 9:4–5)

God has not rejected his people. The Jewish people are the true Israel according to Paul. God's call cannot be lifted. Traditionally Christians have tended to divide people into two groups, believers and nonbelievers. The Jewish people were placed in the second group. But Paul would never feel comfortable with such a neat category for the Israelites according to the flesh. In Paul's metaphorical way of thinking in Rom 11:17, they represent the olive tree. He does not speak of replacement. Instead he describes engraftment, which joins the wild olive shoot to the tree. Moreover, the comparison of the Gentiles to a wild olive branch is not altogether flattering.[22] Clearly the church has not replaced Israel. On the contrary, for Paul the destiny of the church and the synagogue is interrelated in the incomprehensible mystery of the divine purpose. He warns the church, however, against choosing to follow the precarious path of pride. Arrogance has characterized the church's attitude to God's people Israel. Indeed, historically speaking, Christian anti-Semitism always begins with the so-called Jewish rejection of Jesus when Christians cannot tolerate a Jew who refuses to accept Christ. In perspective, however, the Jewish "no" to Jesus is in reality a "yes" to the God of Israel. Christians cannot hate Jews who seek to serve the God of the Bible in good conscience.

Paul understood the relationship more clearly than later church leaders because of his powerful love and personal involvement. As a Jewish theologian from the East, Paul speaks of the relationship between the people of Israel and the followers of Jesus in metaphoric language. His message is clear. Arrogance is not an option for the followers of Jesus.

> But if some of the branches were broken off, and you, a wild olive shoot, were grafted in their place to share the richness of the olive tree, do not boast over the branches. If you do boast, remember it is not you that support the root, but the root that supports you. (Rom 11:17–18)

As Christians, we have often viewed ourselves as the true Israel. We have claimed that the Christians have replaced the Jewish people as God's chosen. Paul teaches a different approach. Engraftment is not the same as replacement.[23] Paul cannot accept God's rejection of his people Israel. On the one hand, the apostle affirms his strong belief in Jesus as Messiah. On the other, he declares that God did not and will not violate his word to the Jewish people. Even Paul's ministry to the Gentiles is based upon his understanding of the root and the branches. While Paul did not believe that God had rejected his people, he was very much aware that many of the faithful within Israel had rejected Jesus.

Perhaps Paul foresaw the danger. The so-called Jewish rejection of Jesus would become the foundation of Christian anti-Judaism. Perhaps he realized that hatred would be generated by the perception that the Jewish people had rejected what is so obvious for the Christian, namely, that Jesus is the fulfillment of messianic expectation in Hebrew prophecy.

Throughout history, Christians have resented Jews because they have not accepted the gospel. Paul recognized the serious nature of the problem. In his wisdom and foresight, Paul warned against such an attitude of arrogance, which he knew would eventually foster hate. Today Christians should realize that many of the Jewish people living in the first century had good reasons for rejecting Jesus. Paul himself was sincere in his rejection of Jesus before the vision on the road to Damascus. John the Baptist himself developed severe skepticism concerning the messiahship of Jesus.[24] Jewish views concerning the messianic idea were diverse, and the words of the Hebrew prophets were always subject to different interpretations. Even in our day and age, some within the Jewish community cannot resolve why so many Jews accepted Jesus in the first century. Nonetheless, wide Jewish acceptance of Jesus as Messiah is a fact of history. Jesus himself defined the meaning of his mission by word and deed in a way that his early disciples could comprehend and follow. In any case, Paul warned the church against ignorant arrogance. His teachings were designed to create genuine love and respect rather than contempt. In the mystery of God, the church and the synagogue are tied one to the other. Not everyone embraced the preaching of Paul, and the apostle could accept this. Paul recognized that when some of the Jewish people rejected his preaching of Jesus, they were really only reaffirming their own strong faith in God. Their "no" to Paul's preaching was not synonymous with a "no" to God almighty. In their minds, they were saying "yes" to God.

Paul's anguish and frustration seem to be directed mainly toward an arrogant church at Rome that was distorting the relationship between Jews and non-Jews. Above all, Paul longed to see this relationship characterized by unconditional love. Love is more powerful than theological dogma and must flow from the heart of faith. Paul was willing to sacrifice a part of his theological integrity in order to achieve the higher goal of unrestricted love. He could agree to disagree on some theological issues in order to pursue the objective of God-like love in his relationship with all people. Indeed, the relationship between Jews and Gentiles occupies a significant portion of Paul's epistle to the church at Rome.[25]

Paul was sensitive to people's backgrounds. In Rom 1:16, when the apostle speaks to the "Jew first and also to the Greek," he recognizes the unique cultural and ethnic heritages of two distinct peoples. The crucial issue for the congregation at Rome revolved around the fellowship of Jew and non-Jew in a culturally biased society. Too often Paul has been read to exclude the Jewish people. A more careful study of Romans would demonstrate that he intended, rather, to include the Gentile. The root supports the branch. The people of Israel have not been replaced, but the Gentile nations have been grafted into the olive tree. For Paul, through Jesus the door had been opened for the Gentiles to reject idolatry and enter into a relationship with the one true God through faith.

Often Rom 10:4 has been translated improperly, "For Christ is the end of the law . . ." The Greek word *telos,* which is translated as "end" in this verse, is better understood in its wider meaning, "goal" or "purpose."[26] Paul viewed the coming of the Messiah as the climax of salvation history. When the New International Version, New American Standard Bible, Revised Standard Version, and King James Version translate the Greek word *telos* with "end," the result is devastating. Instead of stressing the crucial significance of reaching the ultimate goal of Torah, which is indeed foremost in Paul's thought, Christians fall prey to Marcionism: the "end" of the law means license; the law has been canceled and has lost its practical application in living. On the contrary, through Jesus, Paul argued, Torah had reached its objective by bringing the Gentiles into a right relationship with God.[27] Paul is the Jewish apostle to the Gentiles, and the higher purpose of Torah is achieved as the pagan nations reject idolatrous practices and accept Jesus. Through faith they reject idolatry and come into a personal relationship with God. In the mind of Paul, Jesus the Jewish Messiah makes this possible. Earlier in the epistle he declares, "Do we then overthrow the law by this faith? By no means! On the contrary, we uphold the law" (Rom 3:31; cf. Matt 5:17). Paul upholds the goal of Torah. The wild branch has been grafted into the olive tree.

THE MYSTERY

Hence the great mystery involves both Israel and the non-Jews who have been grafted into the tree. Yet in Paul's theology, the mystery also involves the fact that "a hardening has come upon part of Israel." Paul does not explain the mystery. Apparently the apostle could not fully grasp the complexity of all the far-reaching ramifications of the situation. He himself no doubt had experienced personal suffering, intense hardship, immense pain, and emotional stress as a result of his work among the Gentiles. He would cut himself off out of love for his own people (Rom 9:3). In Paul's thought, they are true Israelites, whether they accept Jesus or not. Nonetheless, he offers praise for the depth of God's wisdom. To achieve his higher purpose, God expresses his compassion to all people in need. Paul describes the divine mystery in bold words:

> Lest you be wise in your own conceits, I want you to understand this mystery, brethren: a hardening has come upon part of Israel, until the full number of the Gentiles come in, and so all Israel will be saved. (Rom 11:25–26)

The Christians must learn to love the Jewish people without condition. According to Paul, the people of Israel have not been replaced or rejected. Indeed, in an unfathomable mystery, both the church and the synagogue are inextricably bound together in the final drama of redemption. Paul does not explain it. He merely pronounces a blessing of praise to God because he recognizes that God's way is unsearchable and incomprehensible for the finite human mind (Rom 11:33–36).

The apostle is not a systematic theologian. Paul possesses an Eastern mentality that thrives on contradictions and cherishes the element of mystery in religious faith. In essence, Paul stands in awe and astonishment at the magnitude of God. Let the Master of the universe be God: "To him be glory for ever. Amen" (Rom 11:36).

MARCION OR JESUS?

Since he was a Pharisee, the center of Paul's theology was Torah. After his experience on the road to Damascus, Torah took on new significance because of Jesus. For Paul, Jesus the Jewish Messiah brought a deeper meaning to Torah by his teachings, his life, and his suffering. While it would be wrong to say that Torah had been replaced by Jesus in Paul's theology, the apostle saw Jesus as the culmination of the divine redemptive purpose. Jesus who died will return to complete the messianic task. The drama of salvation is moving toward the goal. Paul affirms the historical teachings of Jesus as well as the redemptive nature of his sufferings on the cross. Jesus died, rose on the third day, and promised to return. Paul even goes so far as to identify with the physical sufferings of Jesus: "I am crucified with Christ" (Gal 2:20). He says that when he is weak, like Jesus who suffered, then he is made strong. The life of Jesus means that God participates with his people in their pain, sharing in their suffering all the while he works to reach the objective of his higher redemptive purpose. Paul was a disciple of Jesus. Jesus brought about the actualization of Torah through his message, model conduct, suffering, and triumph.

While Paul was a disciple of Jesus, Marcion (ca. 130 CE) was a follower of Paul. Marcion, however, distorted the original thrust of Paul's teachings. On the one hand, early church leaders condemned Marcion as a heretic (144 CE), but on the other, they were influenced by his theological reflection. Even today Marcion-like ideas continue to circulate, exerting influence in Christian teachings. The habit of referring to the Hebrew Bible as the Old Testament, so common among Christians, creates the image of obsolescence. The idea that God's grace is first revealed in the New Testament countering the legalism of the old covenant is a dangerous doctrine linked to the heretical theology of Marcion, who rejected the Hebrew Bible and the God of Israel. The Jewish people were despised by God in his teachings. In a similar fashion, many in today's church adamantly contend that the New Covenant (the New Testament) supersedes the Old Covenant (the Hebrew Bible), even though this attitude does not reflect historical orthodoxy. Hence a prominent Christian minister could confidently declare, "God doesn't hear the prayers of a Jew." In such an approach to salvation history, the church has completely replaced the synagogue in God's strategy of redemption. Even Martin Luther described the letter of James as a "right strawy epistle," calling for its removal from the canon because of the message, "So faith by itself, if it has no works, is dead" (Jas 2:17).

Today Judaism is portrayed as teaching a God of wrath, and Christianity, a God of grace. Marcion loved Paul according to his own interpretation of the apostle's teachings—but he hated the Bible. He nullified the divine word spoken to Moses and the Hebrew prophets. For Marcion, Jesus became a revealer of hidden truths. In Marcion's interpretation, it was only in Paul's writings that the truth about grace and works was revealed. In his Bible, he accepted only an edited version of Luke's gospel and ten epistles of Paul. To him the historical life and teachings of Jesus were not relevant. Marcion emphasized knowledge from personal revelation. Knowledge was the way of salvation. When reading Paul, Marcion taught that the law was canceled and that the God of Israel was the evil deity of creation. He longed for the true God of light, a God he supposed had nothing to do with the God of Israel and who was approachable only with the assistance of revelation.

The decisive difference between Marcion and Paul is captured in one word—Jesus. Marcion taught a different way of salvation. His approach had deep roots in anti-Judaism and hatred of the Jewish people. In contrast, Paul makes constant reference to Moses and the prophets and also affirms God's promises to Israel. Paul was a disciple of Jesus because he recognized the authority of his Master's teachings on issues such as marriage and divorce or the observance of the Last Supper. First, Paul affirmed the teaching of Jesus, but he also recognized the deep significance of Jesus' physical sufferings. Moreover, Paul emphasized the message of the early movement of Jesus' disciples. He was not a maverick like Marcion, who rejected all other apostolic teachings. Paul affirmed the tradition that he had received and passed it on to others.

> For I delivered to you as of first importance what I also received, that Christ died for our sins in accordance with the scriptures, that he was buried, and that he was raised on the third day in accordance with the scriptures, and that he appeared to Cephas, then to the twelve. . . . Last of all, as to one untimely born, he appeared also to me. (1 Cor 15:3–9)

Here Paul employs what may be called technical language. In Jewish literature, the verbs *deliver* and *pass on* are used to describe a chain of tradition and how it is preserved from one generation to another.[28] According to traditional Judaism, Moses received the oral teachings of Torah on Mt. Sinai. He delivered what he received to Joshua. Likewise, the oral law has been received and passed on to each subsequent generation.

Paul received a revelation of Jesus the Messiah on the road to Damascus. It was a call to take God's message to the Gentile world. Although Paul received a special revelation of Jesus that was independent of the Jerusalem fellowship of disciples, he still wrote about the tradition that he received, and he passed it on to the congregation at Corinth. Clearly Paul received teachings concerning Jesus from others; in Corinthians, he mentions Cephas, that is, Simeon Peter and the twelve. Paul should not be viewed as an independent freethinker who isolated himself from other leaders in the Jesus movement. Paul's controversial ministry, however, reached out to the pagan world and built bridges between different cultures. The most pressing issue confronting the early movement was what should be required of the new believers from a non-Jewish background. Should they observe the law like Jews and proselytes to Judaism? The issue of the new, non-Jewish believers ultimately had to be decided by the Jerusalem council.

THE JERUSALEM COUNCIL

Because of the success of the mission to the non-Jewish world, social and theological problems erupted within various groups of the early followers of Jesus. Socially it was difficult for Jews and non-Jews to interact with each other. Theologically, the Jewish believers had to determine whether the non-Jews would be required to convert to Judaism in order to follow Jesus. Paul was caught in the middle of the maelstrom. Peter was more ambivalent. The example of Peter will illustrate the problem.

On one occasion, Peter went to Caesarea to visit the home of a Gentile named Cornelius. According to Acts, Peter had to be convinced by a vision to make the trip to a non-Jewish household. In the vision, he was told to eat food that was unclean. When Cornelius's messengers found Peter, he realized that the vision pertained to visiting a Gentile's home. He decided to follow the messengers in spite of his traditional reservations. As a guest of Cornelius, Peter interacted socially with a Gentile who feared God. Though a God fearer, Cornelius had not converted to Judaism. In other words, he had rejected idolatry but had not passed through the whole process of formal conversion, which would have included circumcision. But to Peter's utter amazement, the Spirit fell mightily on uncircumcised men. His response captured the essence of the moment: "Surely no one can refuse water for those to be baptized who have received the Holy Spirit just as we did, can he?" (Acts 10:47). Because of a dramatic demonstration of the Holy Spirit's presence during his visit in this Gentile home, Peter instructed Cornelius to be baptized even though he had not been circumcised.[29] Hence, Cornelius was accepted into the full fellowship of the followers of Jesus without formal conversion to Judaism.

A convert to Judaism had three requirements: he was first required to be circumcised, then to undergo ritual immersion in baptism, and finally to offer a sacrifice in the temple. Peter himself instructed Cornelius to be baptized without circumcision. So, on the one hand, according to Acts, Peter accepted Cornelius without circumcision; but on the other hand, later Peter refused to eat with non-Jewish believers in Antioch. Paul complained about Peter's hypocrisy when he refused to eat with uncircumcised disciples in Antioch. The raging argument came to a head at the Council of Jerusalem. The heart of the problem is described in Acts 15:1: "But some men came down from Judea and were teaching the brethren, 'Unless you are circumcised according to the custom of Moses, you cannot be saved.' "

What is the significance of Acts 15:1? One needs to understand the problem. The council is considering the question of non-Jews. If they are circumcised first, they have undergone conversion to Judaism before being accepted into the full fellowship of the disciples of Jesus. If they have not been circumcised, they are still considered pagan Gentiles. Perhaps they are still worshiping false gods? But there is another status in Jewish thought represented by an individual such as Cornelius: the God fearer. God fearers are referred to in the book of Acts and are mentioned in rabbinic literature. They have not converted to Judaism. But they have rejected all idolatrous practices and have become devoted to the one true God of Israel. In Jewish law, they were not expected to keep all the commandments that the Jewish people observed. They were like the children of Noah. God made a covenant with Noah that focused on the basic moral and ethical requirements that uphold the high spiritual values of the worship of the one true God.

The decision of the Jerusalem council resolved the issue for most of the conservative members of the community, who were stringent in the moral requirements for non-Jews, as well as for the more liberal members of the debate, such as Paul, who desired a more lenient ruling. Moreover, the council's decision is fascinating because of its parallels in Jewish literature. In essence, the council came to a compromise. The decision had roots in Jewish legal discussion. The non-Jews from a pagan background would be viewed more like God fearers than like converts to Judaism. The Apostle Paul and his companion Barnabas, as well as the leaders representing the more conservative side of the issue, such as James and Peter, could reach an agreement to write a letter to the non-Jewish believers: "For it has seemed good to the Holy Spirit and to us to lay upon you no greater burden than these necessary things: that you abstain from what has been sacrificed to idols and from blood and from what is strangled and from unchastity. If you keep yourselves from these, you will do well. Farewell" (Acts 15:28–29). The strongest point of the letter is the reference to avoid idolatrous worship.

In Jewish law there are references to the laws for the children of Noah. In some sources there are seven such laws.[30] But probably the earliest reference to these commandments makes mention of three: idolatry, shedding of blood or murder, and unchastity.[31] People who feared God would obey these fundamental ethical requirements.

One of the greatest of all the commandments was considered to be the fear of the one true God. Perhaps this vital characteristic contributed to the use of the designation "God fearer" in many Jewish sources from late antiquity. The God fearers had rejected the ubiquitous idolatry of the ancient

Greco-Roman world. Because they had abandoned the idolatrous practices of their secular environment, confessed the one true God of Israel, and committed themselves to a moral lifestyle, the God fearers were welcomed into the synagogue. The Jerusalem council did not encourage circumcision for the non-Jew. For an uninitiated person, observance of all the Jewish customs would be too burdensome. For a Pharisee such as Paul, the observance of Torah was integrated into every aspect of daily life and was not a burden, but rather, a delight.

Some important New Testament manuscripts of the decision of the Jerusalem council are even nearer to the Jewish literature. In Codex Bezae, the same three commandments appear as are enumerated in the Jewish sources. The manuscript mentions idolatry, shedding of blood, and unchastity, which are the same three sins as preceded the flood.[32] Codex Bezae also mentions the negative version of the Golden Rule, "Whatsoever you do not want others to do to you, do not do to them." It may be that Codex Bezae represents a more original form of the council's decision. In any case, the outcome of the council was something of a compromise. Paul would probably view these legal requirements as a maximum for the non-Jews to observe. Peter, on the other hand, would tend to view these laws as a minimum. He would hope that the new believers from pagan backgrounds would adopt more of the Jewish religious observance.

The model of Paul in Romans is very instructive. He captured a vision of the mystery of God's higher redemptive purpose. Paul did not want to compromise the sacred identity of the Jewish people by asking the Gentiles to imitate Judaism. In his wisdom, the apostle desired to preserve the special distinctions between Jews and non-Jews as they both worshipped the one true God.[33] Let Jews be Jews and let Gentiles be God fearers! In Paul's teachings, no one possesses an inferior status when the redemptive plan of God is implemented. While Jewish identity is preserved, Paul does not teach inequality. On the contrary, the coming of Jesus creates a powerful invitation to the Gentile nations. The time has come for them to believe in God by faith in the Messiah. Jesus shows them the way. The theology of replacement does not originate with Paul. In the final analysis, Paul preserves the national character and unique distinctions of the Jewish people in their covenantal relationship with God.

PAUL'S CONCEPTUAL APPROACH:
A JEWISH WAY OF THINKING

PAUL'S CONCEPTUAL THEOLOGY
Circular Thought—Not Linear

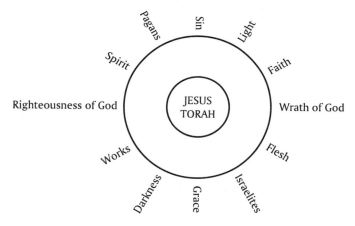

The Concepts are interactive:
in circular thought the conceptual theological ideas
are connected together in continuous motion.
The focal point is Jesus as the goal of Torah.

As a Jewish theologian, Paul pursues a conceptual approach to his teachings. His thought processes are not linear but circular (see above). His theological concepts are interactive. Indeed, they are connected one with another in continuous motion.

Paul's keen intellect works quickly. The apostle understands God and his great love for all humanity as a vibrant whole. One concept belongs to a complex of interactive ideas. Each term he uses to communicate his thought is clustered with other interactive concepts concerning God's relationship to people.

Paul often uses contrasts to express his Jewish theology. The employment of antonyms to define lofty themes is not unusual in early Jewish thought. What is holy? The opposite of profane. What is the good way to which a person should cleave? It is the opposite of the evil way from which a person should flee. What is the good inclination? It is the opposite of the evil inclination. In a similar vein, Paul speaks of the flesh, which for him is the opposite of the spirit. The juxtaposition of terms with opposite meanings is not dualism of the same order as that seen in the Dead Sea Scrolls. Rather, Paul's dualism represents more an antithetical parallelism, which the apostle uses in describing his conceptual approach. Nor is it the same type of dualism found in Gnostic theosophical speculation. Yet Paul would be much closer to the Essenes of the Dead Sea Scrolls than to the Gnostics.[34] The Essenes would never approve, however, of Paul's accommodating approach to the Gentiles. The apostle actively sought the full inclusion of the Gentiles. In sharp contrast, the Essenes believed in double predestination, which is to say that already God has predetermined who will be saved and who will be damned. In other words, with Essene dualism the sons of light and the sons of darkness have already been predetermined. Paul's universal view of God's love is not compatible with the sectarian religious system of Qumran, which even excluded most Jews from the favored lot of the "children of light."[35] The Jewish apostle to the Gentiles calls all people to a loving God who has revealed his goodness in Jesus. Paul endures great hardship to persuade the Gentiles into a decision for God. The gospel is the power of God to the Jew first but also to the Gentiles (Rom 1:16). He contrasts the righteousness of God with the wrath of

God. Paul focuses on God's strategy for the final redemption. He discusses sin as it must be viewed in the context of God's grace, which is made manifest through Jesus.

When the contours of Pauline thought are considered in a cycle of interactive concepts rather than in a straight line where each new idea supersedes and eliminates the previous one, the apostle's conceptual approach to God is given fresh vigor. It is a Jewish way of thinking. Paul, for instance, does not annul Torah by the preaching of grace. Was not the giving of Torah a powerful manifestation of divine grace? In reality, grace and Torah are interrelated. He recognizes that the flesh continues to function even though the power of the spirit is given greater force by faith through the empowerment of the Holy Spirit. He cannot understand the righteousness of God apart from the wrath of God. They have been revealed through the coming of Jesus. Jesus has shown God's righteousness and will demonstrate divine wrath.

The center of Paul's conceptual way of thinking is Jesus, both as he is seen in his life and teachings and as he is revealed in Torah. All of Paul's theological expressions have their origins in his Pharisaic background. As a Pharisee, the central focus of his theology was Torah. From that epicenter he developed all other theological motifs. But with his new belief in the Messiah and his already firm commitment to Torah, the person of Jesus has invaded the epicenter. The notion of a messianic deliverer, it must be remembered, also has its roots in the teachings of the Pharisees. Even while focusing on Jesus, Paul did not see a break in the continuity of his thinking from his Hebrew heritage as a Pharisee. Now he has received a special task because of his call to preach to the Gentiles. Paul's destiny was rooted in the visions of the old Hebrew prophets. At least some of them foresaw the day when the Gentile nations would serve God. The Apostle Paul told his story to the Jew first but also to the Greek. He was the apostle to the Gentiles, and he glories in his call. His career was based upon the foundation of calling the pagan nations to a new understanding of the one true God of Israel through faith in Jesus the Jewish Messiah.

At this juncture we discover the major distinctions between Jesus and Paul. Jesus spoke to his people living in the land of Israel. He would have taught them primarily in Hebrew (and/or Aramaic). Jesus was provincial. Paul was international. The apostle worked outside the land of Israel, teaching and preaching in Greek. Jesus spoke to the Jews. Paul, on the other hand, spoke mainly to the Gentiles. Nonetheless, both Jesus and Paul possessed a high view of Torah. Gospel teachings such as the Sermon on the Mount indicate that Jesus had a far superior understanding of Torah.[36] His educational background in Hebrew literature and oral tradition greatly surpassed that of the Apostle Paul. But Torah gave Jesus and Paul a common bond. In contrast to Jesus, Paul's epicenter of Torah had absorbed a new and powerful theological component. The messianic idea as it revolves around the person of Jesus became dominant in Paul's thinking. The Messiah had come. Both Jesus as the anointed one of God and Torah occupy the position of centrality for the theology of the Apostle Paul. He is called to preach the message of Jesus the Messiah to the Gentile nations. Paul may indeed be described as a Pharisee, a Jewish theologian living among the diverse groups of early Christians in the Greco-Roman world. He was trying to bring the Jews and non-Jews tightly together into the circle of early Christian community through a more meaningful relationship one with the other, based upon their common faith in God, the message of Jesus, and the teachings contained within the Hebrew Bible.

PAUL THE JEWISH THEOLOGIAN: NOTES

1. See W. C. van Unnik, *Tarsus or Jerusalem* (London: Epworth, 1962) 32–33. On the basis of the three verbs in Acts 22:3—"brought up,"

"educated," and "being zealous"—as well as Paul's own words in Phil 3:4–5, van Unnik is correct in stressing Paul's educational and cultural background in the Jewish city of Jerusalem. Indeed, it is only from Acts that we learn that Paul's birthplace was Tarsus. The apostle himself never mentions this detail of his life in his own writings. For him, it was not worth mentioning. Paul's heritage is a source of great debate. See H. J. Schoeps, *Paul: The Theology of the Apostle in the Light of Jewish Religious History* (Philadelphia: Westminster, 1961); W. D. Davies, *Paul and Rabbinic Judaism* (New York: Harper, 1948); and the very important work of Sanders, *Paul and Palestinian Judaism.*

2. The purely Hellenistic approach, which divorces Paul from his Jewish background, must lose favor among scholars when the issues surrounding his epistles are understood properly. Paul's solutions to problems are anchored in Torah and the teachings of Jesus. Hence, Schoeps, *Paul,* 48, has rightly observed, "The talk of Paul's acute Hellenization of Christianity which has sprung up in consequence of the Tübingen school must, however, be rejected, for this phenomenon is post-Pauline only, and its first signs are to be found in the Deutero-Pauline writings." See also Davies, *Paul and Rabbinic Judaism,* 323, who concluded, "The gospel of Paul was not the annulling of Judaism but its completion, and as such it took up into itself the essential genius of Judaism."

3. Cf. S. Sandmel, *The Genius of Paul* (New York: Schocken, 1970) 1: "Paul was a religious genius. In that eminence his position is secure from the assaults of his detractors. . . . Some opponents wanted to discredit the man, but others sought to distort not Paul but his teachings."

4. See Jakob Jonsson, *Humour and Irony in the New Testament* (Leiden: Brill, 1985) 223.

5. See David Flusser, "The Dead Sea Sect and Pre-Pauline Christianity," in *Judaism and the Origins of Christianity* (Jerusalem: Magnes, 1988) 23–74; cf. Flusser's Hebrew discussion, "Paulinism in Paul," in *Yahadut Umekorot Hanatzrut* (Tel Aviv: Sifriyat Hapoalim, 1979) 359–80.

6. See the *Acts of Paul* 2.3, in *The Apocryphal New Testament* (ed. M. R. James; Oxford: Clarendon, 1980) 273; cf. the revised edition, *The Apocryphal New Testament* (ed. J. K. Elliott; Oxford: Clarendon, 1993) 364.

7. See also Acts 21:39; 22:3. Cf. Stendahl, *Paul Among Jews and Gentiles.*

8. Strabo, *Geography* 14.5.15, in *The Geography of Strabo* (LCL; trans. H. L. Jones; Cambridge: Harvard University, 1960) 6.347. Strabo observes that it was not unusual for a native of Tarsus to study abroad.

9. See Acts 5:34–39, where Gamaliel ardently defends the apostles. Many people in Jerusalem supported the apostles against the attempts of the

Sadducees to arrest them (Acts 5:17). See Acts 5:26, where the police who arrested Peter and the apostles feared being stoned by the people, many of whom were probably Pharisees who opposed the actions of the priests and the Sadducees.

10. The declaration of the Pharisees regarding Paul, "We find nothing wrong in this man," should not surprise the serious historian of the Second Temple period even if it might shock the student of the history of the relationship between the church and the synagogue.

11. See, e.g., Rom 1:2. Cf. 2 Tim 3:16; 2 Timothy is one of the Pastoral Epistles, which many scholars have argued are derived from Paul's followers. In his epistles, Paul also makes use of the sayings of Jesus as a source of authority in the life of the community.

12. Paul compelled Timothy to be circumcised when he accompanied Paul and Silas. Although Timothy's father was Greek, his mother was Jewish. In Jewish law, the mother determines the legal status of the child. Since Timothy's mother was Jewish, according to the religious law of the halakah Timothy also would be considered Jewish. On the other hand, Paul would not ask a non-Jew to be circumcised (Acts 16:1–3).

13. Gal 5:14. Hillel, the grandfather of Paul's teacher Gamaliel, taught a similar principle; see *b. Šabb.* 31a and parallels. On Hillel and his teachings see Nahum Glatzer, *Hillel the Elder: The Emergence of Classical Judaism* (New York: B'nai B'rith Hillel Foundations, 1956); and Yitzhak Buxbaum, *The Life and Teachings of Hillel* (London: Jason Aronson, 1994). The positive version of the Golden Rule is the summary of Torah and the prophets in Matthew's version of the commandment (Matt 7:12).

14. Alan Segal, *Paul the Convert* (New Haven: Yale University, 1990) 206. Segal has grasped the paradoxical situation with insight, but I believe that the apostle would probably be offended by his designation "a former Pharisee," because Paul considered himself to be a Pharisee.

15. Cf. the important discussion of Raymond E. Brown, "The Roman Church near the End of the First Christian Generation," in Raymond E. Brown and J. Meier, *Antioch and Jerusalem* (New York: Paulist, 1983) 105–27.

16. See David Flusser, "A New Sensitivity in Judaism and the Christian Message," in *Judaism and the Origins of Christianity*, 469–93.

17. Perhaps there is a touch of the modern Jewish philosopher and rabbi Abraham Joshua Heschel in Paul. Both the Apostle Paul and Heschel seemed to feel a sense of wonder at the mystery of God. Cf. the thought-provoking studies by Heschel, e.g., *God in Search of Man: A Philosophy of*

GOSHEN COLLEGE LIBRARY
GOSHEN, INDIANA

Judaism (New York: Farrar, Straus and Cudahy, 1955); *The Insecurity of Freedom* (Philadelphia: Jewish Publication Society, 1966); and *The Prophets* (New York: Harper & Row, 1962).

18. See Max Kadushin, *A Conceptual Approach to the Mekilta* (New York: Jewish Theological Seminary, n.d.) 7, where he explores the kingdom-of-heaven theme. Kadushin has discussed the methodology of the rabbis more extensively in some of his other works, e.g., *The Rabbinic Mind* (2d ed.; New York: Blaisdell, 1965); and *The Theology of Seder Eliahu: A Study in Organic Thinking* (New York, 1932). On the kingdom, cf. Gösta Lundström, *The Kingdom of God in the Teaching of Jesus* (Richmond, Va.: John Knox, 1963); and Brad H. Young, *Jesus and His Jewish Parables* (New York: Paulist, 1989) 189–235.

19. See Schoeps, *Paul*, 49.

20. After all, Isaiah spoke of the temple as a house of prayer for all peoples and conceived of the Jewish people as a light to the Gentiles. Zechariah envisioned the day when the Gentile would grasp the coattail of the Jew and be led up to the temple of the Lord for worship. See also Lloyd Gaston, *Paul and the Torah* (Vancouver: University of British Columbia, 1987) 116–34; cf. Edward Schillebeeckx, *Paul the Apostle* (New York: Crossroad, 1983) 26.

21. See Rom 9:3; cf. Moses in Exod 32:32. Paul uses the Greek term *anathema*, which has a wide range of meanings. Paul would make himself an *anathema* for his brothers and sisters in Israel who do not believe in Jesus. He would give himself for them. Often this is understood as accepting eternal damnation. While the apostle seems willing to do anything, even sacrifice himself, for his people, it is quite likely that the word *anathema* here does not mean suffering in the fire of hell forever but, rather, a change in spiritual status. The word, like its Hebrew equivalent *cherem*, can refer to something dedicated to God (see Luke 21:5); cf. W. Bauer, W. Arndt and F. W. Gingrich, F. Danker, *A Greek-English Lexicon of the New Testament and Early Christian Literature* (2d ed.; Chicago: University of Chicago, 1979). Paul would be setting himself apart from Jesus, i.e., cutting himself off from the Messiah (cf. 1 Cor 16:22). He would not, however, annul the blessings promised by God to the Israelites (Rom 10:4f.). After all, the apostle affirms God's faithfulness to his people in Rom 11:26, "and so all Israel will be saved." As James Dunn observed, "The climax will be the fulfillment of his [Paul's] heart's prayer (10:1)—Israel's salvation, Israel's restoration to full communion with its God. Whatever is happening to Israel now, Paul has been given the divinely revealed assurance that all will come out right for Israel in the end, that God's faithfulness to his first love will be demonstrated for all to see." See James D. G. Dunn, *Romans 9–16* (WBC; Dallas:

Word, 1988) 691–93. On the use of the term *anathema* in 1 Cor 16:22, see the excellent commentary by Gordon Fee, *The First Epistle to the Corinthians* (Grand Rapids: Eerdmans, 1987) 837–39.

22. The Gentiles are an amorphous group committing sin, denying God, and persecuting the Jewish people. But the ancient Hebrew prophets envisioned a day when Gentiles would come to faith in the one true God. Paul's intense love for the diverse Gentile nations is a genuine expression of this old prophetic vision.

23. Cf. Marvin Wilson, *Our Father Abraham* (Grand Rapids: Eerdmans, 1989) 3–18.

24. Matt 11:2; Luke 7:19. See Brad H. Young, "The Kingdom Breaks Forth or the Kingdom Suffers Violence?" in *Jesus the Jewish Theologian* (Peabody, Mass.: Hendrickson, 1995). Cf. also David Flusser, *Jesus* (New York: Herder and Herder, 1969) 84–92.

25. Markus Barth, *The People of God* (Sheffield, England: University of Sheffield, 1983) 72, has observed, "Even by taking offence at Jesus Christ and rejecting the gospel, the Jews render the church a service for which she owes it gratitude, love and respect. Without the Jewish people there is no church. Conversely, the church is a detour for the salvation of Israel. Where men meant to do evil, God meant to do good. . . . With the complete physical extinction of all Jews from the face of the earth the demonstration and proof of God's existence would collapse and the church would lose its *raison d'etre*: the church would fall. The future of the church lies in the salvation of all Israel."

26. See Hendrikus Boers, "The Problem of Jews and Gentiles in the Macro-Structure of Romans," *Svensk Exegetisk Årsbok* 47 (1982) 187.

27. George Howard, "Christ the End of the Law: The Meaning of Romans 10 4ff.," *Journal of Biblical Literature* 88 (1969) 331–37, observed, "Christ is the goal of the law to everyone who believes, because the ultimate goal of the law is that all nations are to be blessed in Abraham. The passage is one of the greatest of Paul's statements concerning his doctrine of the inclusion of the gentiles. In fact, it is becoming increasingly clear that this doctrine permeates the entirety of his letter to the Romans" (337). This is a foundational study of Paul's main thesis in Romans. Cf. also R. David Kaylor, *Paul's Covenant Community: Jew and Gentile in Romans* (Atlanta: John Knox, 1988) 159–93; and J. Christian Beker, *Paul the Apostle: A Triumph of God in Life and Thought* (Philadelphia: Fortress, 1980) 85.

28. See, e.g., the language of ʾ*Abot* 1:1: "Moses received the Torah from Sinai and passed it on to Joshua and Joshua to the elders and the elders to the Prophets; and the Prophets . . ."

29. This description is a fine example of how the wall dividing Jews and Gentiles was brought down in early Christianity. Paul and his disciples would certainly agree. Cf. Eph 2:14–15: "who has made us both one, and has broken down the dividing wall of hostility, by abolishing in his flesh the law of commandments." Through death to the flesh, the Christian is made free to follow the teachings of the Bible with the empowerment of the Holy Spirit. The death of Jesus brings unity for all peoples in the plan of redemption. Cf. M. Barth, *Ephesians* (AB 34–34A; Garden City, N.Y.: Doubleday, 1982) 1.260–65; and J. Gnilka, *Der Epheserbrief* (Freiburg: Herder, 1982) 138–43.

30. See, e.g., *b. Sanh.* 56a: "Our rabbis taught: Seven precepts were the sons of Noah commanded: social laws; to refrain from blasphemy; idolatry; adultery; bloodshed; robbery; and eating flesh cut from a living animal."

31. See *Jub.* 7:21, where three categories of sins are said to have brought about the flood. See R. H. Charles, *The Book of Jubilees* (Oxford: Clarendon, 1902) 61.

32. The variant manuscript text according to Codex Bezae on Acts 15:20b reads, "to abstain from pollutions of idols, from fornication, from blood[shed] and whatsoever you would that men should not do to you do not to another." (Similar readings according to Bezae appear in Acts 15:29b and 21:25.) See also A. Resch, "Das Aposteldekret nach seiner ausserkanonischen Textgestalt untersucht," in *Texte und Untersuchungen* (new series; Leipzig, 1905) 3.1–179; David Flusser and Shmuel Safrai, "Das Aposteldekret und die Noachitischen Gebote," in *"Wer Tora vermehrt, mehrt Leben": Festgabe für Heinz Kremers zum 60. Geburtstag* (ed. E. Brocke and H. J. Barkenings; Neukirchen: Vluyn, 1986) 173–92; and David Flusser, "Paul's Jewish-Christian Opponents in the Didache," in *Gilgul: Essays on Transformation, Revolution, and Permanence in the History of Religions, Dedicated to R. J. Zwi Werblowski* (ed. S. Shaked, D. Shulman, and G. Stroumsa; Leiden: Brill, 1987) 71–90. On the negative version of the Golden Rule, see *The Authorized Daily Prayer Book* (ed. Joseph H. Hertz; New York: Bloch, 1948) 644f.

33. In Gal 3:28 Paul declares, "There is neither Jew nor Greek, there is neither slave nor free, there is neither male nor female; for you are all one in Christ Jesus." While the apostle does not teach inequality, he recognizes ethnic and cultural distinctives. He can rejoice in the differences. The apostle maintains Jewish identity within the joining together of diverse peoples in Jesus (see Gal 5:3). True unity means rich diversity within the divine purpose.

34. See Flusser, "The Dead Sea Scrolls." Flusser's brilliant study shows the beginnings of Christianity in two strata that are understood in the light of the Dead Sea Scrolls.

35. Cf. P. Benoit, "Qumran and the New Testament," in *Paul and the Dead Sea Scrolls* (ed. J. Murphy O'Connor and J. Charlesworth; New York: Crossroad, 1990) 1–30.

36. See David Flusser, *Jewish Sources in Early Christianity* (Tel Aviv: MOD, 1989) 19, 62.

3 Pentecost, the Nations of the World, and the Apostle Paul

The Spirit is not only the one who teaches us to stand in this childlike relationship to God and to pronounce steadfastly the name Father in spite of all that still raises itself against this relationship; he is also the one who maintains this living communion. He comes from God to awaken in the hearts of God's people the true consciousness of children, but he also mounts up, as it were, from the hearts of the children to God, because in their inability to find the right words in prayer he enters in for them with unutterable groanings; and God, the great searcher of hearts will judge them according to this holy intention of the Spirit which is acceptable to God (Rom 8:26ff.).

Herman Ridderbos
Paul: An Outline of His Theology

PEOPLE from "every nation under heaven" gathered in Jerusalem to celebrate the festival of Pentecost. Paul was the Jewish apostle who traveled throughout the nations of the world with incredible energy and zeal. Paul went out of Jerusalem to the world, but Pentecost brought the world to Jerusalem. The festival in the book of Acts marked a major upheaval in the experience of the early followers of Jesus. The event signaled a decisive transition as Jews and proselytes from around the known world gathered in Jerusalem to celebrate the feast.

For Christians, the Jewish celebration of the feast of Pentecost in first-century Jerusalem commemorates the occasion when the Holy Spirit empowered the early followers of Jesus to serve God with renewed vigor and dedication to his teachings. For Christians, Pentecost means divine empowerment for service. For the Jewish people, Pentecost is the time when God gave Torah to Israel. In the biblical period, it was a harvest festival of great rejoicing. Now archaeology has revealed fresh insight concerning the birth of the church. The monumental stairway leading up to the temple and extensive baptismal pools *(mikvaot)* have been discovered. Rabbinic literature, moreover, sheds light on the meaning of Pentecost in ancient Judaism. Pentecost is sacred to both Christians and Jews. At Pentecost, God's people received the word of God and the power of the Holy Spirit. Pentecost must be viewed through the prism of Jerusalem, archaeology, and rabbinic literature. It signaled a world outreach as the disciples began to bear witness from Jerusalem to the uttermost parts of the world (Acts 1:8; cf. Isa 49:6). In Acts, Paul fulfilled this task by taking the message of God's kingdom to the imperial capital, Rome, a city that would seem like the "ends of the earth" for many first-century Jews.

During Pentecost, Judaism celebrates the giving of Torah—God's revelation to his beloved people. Some leading scholars have claimed that Pentecost became associated with the giving of Torah only after the rise of Christianity.[1] On the one hand, it is true that the Old Testament does not link Pentecost with the giving of Torah. This concept arose within Jewish interpretations of the event. Yet Moshe Weinfeld of the Bible department of the Hebrew University has decisively argued that Pentecost was already associated with the giving of the law in the time of Jesus.[2] He points out that the idea of covenant and covenant renewal at Pentecost appears in the book of *Jubilees* and the Dead Sea Scrolls, indicating that already in the second century BCE these concepts had gained acceptance. In Torah, God's way is made known. Judaism celebrates God's revelation during the festival of Pentecost. By the time of Jesus and the writing of the book of Acts, the idea that Pentecost was the time when God gave Torah to his people already seems to have become firmly established. As we will see, even the descriptions of the revelation of Torah on Mount Sinai for Israel and the pneumatic empowerment for the church on the Temple Mount correspond to each other with remarkable lucidity.

Christianity celebrates the birth of the church in renewed vigor when she remembers how the Holy Spirit was poured out on the day of Pentecost. The Spirit empowers people for God's work. Jerusalem is the place where it all happened. In the Jewish temple in the holy city of Jerusalem, God commanded an ingathering of his people: "Three times a year all your males shall appear before the LORD your God at the place which he will choose [Jerusalem]: at the feast of unleavened bread [Passover], at the feast of weeks [Pentecost], and at the feast of booths [Tabernacles]" (Deut 16:16). Like Passover and Tabernacles, Pentecost became associated with Israel's wilderness experience.

Passover tells the story of God's deliverance. The people were slaves in Egypt until God delivered them out of the house of bondage unto his great liberty. Sukkot, the Feast of Tabernacles (or Booths), is also one of the great pilgrimage festivals. Sukkot celebrates God's provision for the people during their desert wanderings. They lived in *sukkot,* that is, temporary dwellings or tabernacles; and they depended on the Lord for his provision each day. The cloud provided cover for the Israelites by day; the fire guided and protected them by night. God provided the manna for food throughout the journey. He brought quail and gave them water. The tent dwellers in the wilderness experienced God's miraculous care. The pilgrim festivals, Passover and Tabernacles, recall God's deliverance from slavery and his providential care in the wilderness. As during Passover and Tabernacles, during the festival of Pentecost the people of God were commanded to make a pilgrimage to Jerusalem. Consequently, it was natural to view Pentecost as signifying the events associated with Passover and Tabernacles.

This pilgrimage festival of Pentecost was understood by the Jewish sages as the next stage in the journey of the ancient Israelites. They had been saved from slavery at Passover. They had been preserved in their desert wanderings in *sukkot*. Now the people of Israel came to Mount Sinai. Accompanied by peals of thunder and bursts of lightning, God's awesome presence was made known as he revealed his will to the people he loved (Exod 19–20). God's revelation in Torah was given to his people. Pentecost is the "time in which God gave us our Torah" *(zeman natan toratenu)*.

As one of the three major pilgrim festivals commanded by God, the celebration of Pentecost has beckoned untold multitudes to Jerusalem throughout the centuries. Acts 2:8–12 mentions people from all over the world who came from different cultures, speaking languages foreign to the inhabitants of the land of Israel. In some ways, the event is a foreshadowing of Paul's Christian witness to the Gentiles. All of the people, whether Jewish by birth, God fearers, or converts to Judaism, were bound together in faith. They had gathered into Jerusalem to give thanks for God's blessings. The book of Acts describes how the early Christians were filled with the Holy Spirit and spoke with other tongues:

> When the day of Pentecost had come, they were all together in one place. And suddenly a sound came from heaven like the rush of mighty wind, and it filled all the house where they were sitting. And there appeared to them tongues as of fire, distributed and resting on each one of them. And they began to speak in other tongues, as the Spirit gave them utterance. (Acts 2:1–4)

The followers of Jesus were gathered together in one accord (Greek, *homothymadon*, Acts 1:14) for this awesome event. The unity of the early church during this decisive period of her history paved the way for the collective experience of the Holy Spirit (Acts 2:1, 46). Only through supernatural power would the message of Israel's one true God being revealed in the life and ministry of Jesus be heard among the Gentiles. In a similar way, the rabbinic tradition stresses the unity of the people of Israel before they received the gift of Torah:

> Great is peace, for with regard to all the journeyings it is written, "And the children of Israel journeyed [plural] . . . and encamped" [plural] (Num. xxxiii, 5 *et passim*), [the plural number implying that] they journeyed in dissension, and they encamped in dissension. When, however, they all came before Mount Sinai, they all became one encampment. This is indicated by what is written, "And there Israel encamped [sing.] before the mount" (Ex. xix, 2). It is written here not "And the children of Israel encamped" [plural], but "Israel encamped" [sing.]. Said the Holy One, blessed be: "This is the hour at which I am giving Torah to My children."[3]

The people of Israel were in one accord, without dissension, when the Torah was given at Mount Sinai. When the community of faith is of one accord, it acts like a magnet to attract the divine presence. The motif seems to be a part of the background imagery employed in Acts to describe the giving of the Holy Spirit to the church.

Although Christians have often associated "the house" in Acts 2:2 with the upper room in Acts 1:13, it is much more likely that the site of the miracle of Pentecost was the temple. The mention of "the house" most probably referred to the house of the Lord, where they would have been sitting for the study of Torah. The temple was the meeting place of God's people for the Feast of Pentecost. In Acts 2:46, they gathered in the temple with one accord each day to pray, study, and learn.

Archaeology has revealed another link between the Pentecost experience of the church and the temple. The recently excavated monumental stairway that led up to a wide platform area may well have been the meeting place of the early believers. Pious pilgrims would ritually immerse in baptismal pools and ascend the steps to the platform, where they could enter through the Hulda gates into the portico of the temple. These spacious areas served as meeting places for the study of Torah. Perhaps the early Christians were gathered on this platform or in one of the study halls of the temple when the Holy Spirit fell upon them.

The whole place was shaken with the divine presence. These descriptive terms from Acts echo the theophany of God at Sinai when the Torah was given to Israel. They recall the awesome glory of the Lord that later filled the holy temple when it was dedicated. The temple was filled with the divine presence: "The house, the house of the LORD was filled with a cloud, so that the priests could not stand to minister because of the cloud; for the glory of the LORD filled the house of God" (2 Chron 5:14).

Pilgrims and proselytes from all over the world heard the early Christians speaking in foreign languages. The people of these lands understood the message concerning the wonderful works of God. The miracle was in the speaking. Even though the apostles had never learned these languages, they spoke to the visitors to Jerusalem in their native dialects. Tongues of fire appeared above the heads of the early Christians as they spoke. Then Peter preached a message about Jesus. Three thousand people believed and wanted to be baptized. Now with the excavations of the Temple Mount, forty-eight ritual immersion baths have been uncovered.[4] Some archaeologists have estimated that two hundred baptismal pools may have served the enormous masses of pilgrims who would enter the temple to worship God. During the feasts of Israel, many baptismal pools were required to service the crowds of pilgrims. These ritual immersion baths must have been the actual baptismal pools used by the apostles in the mass baptism on the day of Pentecost.

In biblical days, Pentecost commemorated the firstfruits of the grain harvests. In Jewish culture, harvest time is an occasion for joyous celebration. The people of God recognize the divine favor. The farmers must do their work, but God gives the produce for harvest. Pentecost occurred on the fiftieth day after Passover: "And you shall count from the morrow after the sabbath, from the day that you brought the sheaf of the wave offering; seven full weeks shall they be, counting fifty days to the morrow after the seventh sabbath; then you shall present a cereal offering of new grain to the LORD" (Lev 23:15–16). The celebration of Pentecost was marked by great joy.

As has been seen, all three pilgrimage festivals are connected with God's redemption. Passover commemorates the salvation of the people from Egypt, and Tabernacles recalls God's miraculous provision in the wilderness. Pentecost is another crucial stop in the journey to the promised land. It was natural for the feast to be connected with the giving of the Torah from Mount Sinai during the desert experience of the people of Israel. In their wilderness wanderings, the people were overwhelmed with God's glory when he revealed the Torah to Moses (Exod 19–20).

In rabbinic literature, the powerful word of God was compared to a hammer striking an anvil, with sparks flying out from the force of the blow. When the word poured forth from the mouth of the Almighty, fiery sparks flew in every direction—symbolizing that each divine utterance was heard in every language. They were like tongues of fire. The divine revelation of Torah flowed out, bestowing illumination upon the people of God. God's will and way had been revealed.

> Rabbi Johanan said: "What is meant by the verse, 'The LORD gives the word: They that publish the tidings are a great host? (Psalm 68:12).' Every single word that went forth from the Omnipresent was split up into seventy languages." The school of Ishmael taught: "And like a hammer that breaks the rocks in sparks so every single

word that went forth from the Holy One, blessed be He, split up into seventy languages."[5]

The mention of seventy languages is symbolic. The rabbis believed that it referred to all the languages of the world. Acts 2:5 stresses that "devout men from every nation under heaven" had gathered in Jerusalem to celebrate Pentecost. The description of sparks of fire, moreover, corresponds to the tongues of fire mentioned in Acts.

The first-century Jewish philosopher Philo of Alexandria described the words of God at Mount Sinai in a similar way. The mention of tongues of fire in Acts brought to remembrance the awesome appearance of God when he revealed Torah. Philo recounts the divine energy and the fire that accompanied the giving of the law:

> Then from the midst of the fire that streamed from heaven there sounded forth to their utter amazement a voice, for the flame became articulate speech in the language familiar to the audience, and so clearly and distinctly were the words formed by it that they seemed to see them rather than hear them.[6]

The words of Torah appeared to the people in fire. They saw the flames and heard the voice in their own language. The tongues of fire in the book of Acts are paralleled by Jewish descriptions of the theophany at Sinai.

For Christians, Pentecost means divine empowerment for God's purpose. The liturgical church remembers the miracle of Pentecost in the prayers and Bible readings of Whitsunday.[7] Jesus had promised the early believers power to fulfill his teachings. Most Christians stand in awe when reading the account of Acts 2, which describes the church's encounter with the power of the Holy Spirit. The place was shaken. Visitors from all parts of the world who had made pilgrimage to Jerusalem heard the early Christians speaking about the wonderful works of God in the different languages of the nations.

They witnessed the tongues of fire resting on the heads of those filled with the Spirit. The church was empowered to fulfill her purpose in bringing hope and help to people in need. She was called to bear witness to God's love. The Apostle Paul became her emissary to the pagan nations of the world.

Pentecost is thus a point of convergence where the spiritual force of God's blessing has dramatically impacted both Judaism and Christianity. While the name itself simply means fifty days, referring to the seven weeks plus one day for the harvest of grains, for Jews and Christians, Pentecost has come to signify the giving of divine revelation on Mount Sinai—the zenith of God's self-disclosure in Torah for Israel—as well as the outpouring of the Holy Spirit for the church. The people of the synagogue and the church are able to join hands together at Pentecost and recognize God's goodness for his people. The harvest festival became the main occasion when the Jewish people living in the land and those coming from the distant parts of the Diaspora celebrated God's blessings in providing food and meeting other needs. Josephus tells how the city was crowded with the country folk from the surrounding region.[8] In many ways, it is the city of Jerusalem that draws the nations of the world together. Pilgrimage to the city changes the people who come. Encountering Jerusalem leads to a deeper spiritual experience. For the apostle to the Gentiles, Pentecost signaled a major transition that had prepared the way for Paul's outreach to the nations of the world.

Pentecost possesses special significance for the Christian and Jewish communities of faith. Jerusalem is the city where the spiritual streams of Judaism and Christianity converge. The gift of Torah brings challenge. The outpouring of the Holy Spirit calls for service. The description of Pentecost in the book of Acts is designed to recall the giving of Torah and the shaking of the temple at its dedication.[9] The rabbinic literature shows how tongues of fire representing the seventy nations of the world were used to describe the revelation of

Torah. These tongues of fire are similar to the description of the day of Pentecost in Acts 2, when the church was empowered to serve.

In Acts, Pentecost means empowerment to serve others in need and bear witness to God's favor. Torah's revelation and the Holy Spirit's fire revive the faithful to meet the challenge. It is the time of Torah's revelation and the outpouring of the Holy Spirit. Pentecost means spiritual renewal and revitalization for the people of God. It prepared the way for the call of the Apostle Paul, who gave testimony of God's goodness to the pagan Gentiles.

Pentecost is the backdrop of Paul's ministry to the nations of the world. The words of Jesus are not intended for his people alone. A Pharisee educated in Jerusalem must bring the message of Israel's one God and his Messiah to the Gentiles.

PENTECOST, THE NATIONS OF THE WORLD, AND THE APOSTLE PAUL: NOTES

1. See, e.g., Louis Jacobs, "Shavuot," *Encyclopaedia Judaica* (Jerusalem: Keter, 1972) vol. 14, col. 1320. The issue is complex, and some of the greatest Jewish scholars have linked the dating of Pentecost with the giving of the law long after the Second Temple period.

2. Moshe Weinfeld, "Pentecost as Festival of the Giving of the Law," *Immanuel* 8 (1978) 7–18.

3. *Lev. Rab.* 9:9; see the critical Hebrew edition of M. Margulies, *Midrash Vayikra Rabbah* (Jerusalem: Wahrmann Books, 1970) 1.189; and the English translation in *Midrash Rabbah* (London: Soncino, 1939) 4.115. Cf. also *Lev. Rab.* 19:4.

4. Meir Ben Dov, *In the Shadow of the Temple* (Jerusalem: Keter, 1982); on ritual baths, see pp. 150–53; on the monumental stairway on the southern end of the temple, see pp. 108–13. See also Nahman Avigad, *Discovering Jerusalem* (Jerusalem: Israel Exploration Society, 1980) 139–43.

5. *B. Šabb.* 88a and parallels. See Weinfeld, "Pentecost as Festival," 14–15; cf. P. Billerbeck, *Das Kommentar zum Neuen Testament aus Talmud und Midrasch* (Munich: C.H. Beck, 1978) 2.597–606.

6. See Philo, *Decal.* 46, in *Philo* (LCL; trans. F. H. Colson; Cambridge, Mass.: Harvard University, 1968) 7.28–29. On speaking in tongues in the New Testament, cf. Stendahl, *Paul Among Jews and Gentiles,* 109–24.

7. See J. Daniélou, *The Bible and the Liturgy* (Notre Dame, Ind.: University of Notre Dame, 1956) 319–32.

8. Josephus, *J.W.* 1.253; *Ant.* 14.337.

9. See Exod 19–20; 2 Chron 5:2–14; cf. Richard Steven Notley, "The Concept of the Holy Spirit in Jewish Literature of the Second Temple Period and Pre-Pauline Christianity" (diss., Hebrew University, Jerusalem, 1991) 262–303.

Judaism and Christianity: Diverse Perspectives on Torah

The spiritual alienation from Israel is most forcefully
expressed in the teaching of Marcion, who affirmed the
contrariety and abrupt discontinuity between the God of the
Hebrew Bible and the God whom Jesus had come to reveal.
Marcion wanted a Christianity free from any vestige of
Judaism. He saw his task as that of showing the complete
opposition between the Hebrew Bible and the Gospels.
Although in the year 144 of the Christian era the church
expelled the apostle of discontinuity and anathematized his
doctrines, Marcion remains a formidable menace, a satanic
challenge. In the modern Christian community the power of
Marcionism is much more alive and widespread than is
generally realized. . . . According to Rudolf Bultmann (as
summarized by Bernhard W. Anderson), "for the Christian
the Old Testament is not revelation, but is essentially
related to God's revelation in Christ as hunger is to food and
despair is to hope. . . . The God who spoke to Israel no longer
speaks to us in the time of the new Covenant." Here is the
spiritual resurrection of Marcion. Was not the God of Israel
the God of Jesus? How dare a Christian substitute his own
conception of God for Jesus' understanding of God and still
call himself a Christian!

Abraham Joshua Heschel
The Insecurity of Freedom

JESUS taught that he came to fulfill the law (Matt 5:17), Paul
that he placed the Torah on a firmer footing (Rom 3:31),
but Marcion that the Old Testament had been fulfilled in the

divine revelation of Jesus and therefore had become irrelevant for the Christian.[1] In the preceding chapter, we have seen the crucial significance of these diverse perspectives on Torah for the very foundations of Judaism and Christianity. Christianity and Judaism define themselves largely on the basis of how they characterize Torah.[2] For Christianity, the question continues to reverberate: Was the Jewish Torah fulfilled by Jesus in such a way as to undermine its practical meaning?

The significance of Torah for both Jesus and Paul emanates from Judaism. Jewish faith views the giving of Torah as a supernatural event of utmost import.[3] God descended from heaven to Mount Sinai in order to reveal his will to Israel. Christianity, on the other hand, views the law through the window of ecclesiastical history. This perspective, to a certain degree, has been influenced by Christianity's struggle to define itself apart from its Jewish roots.[4] At the forefront of that struggle have been influential figures such as Marcion (ca. 85–159 CE), who denied the validity of the Hebrew Bible for Christian faith and practice. Christendom fought against Marcion and his pervasive theology. Even though the church declared Marcion a heretic, his view of the law is sometimes tolerated or even embraced, while the Jewish understanding of Torah is ignored. The Jewish view of Torah, however, was the foundation of the early Christian theology.

In contrast to Marcion, Jesus and Paul valued Torah.[5] Here we will examine the words of Jesus in Matt 5:17 and of Paul in Rom 3:31.[6] The deep roots of these two key verses in Judaism are sometimes overlooked. When this happens, our opinions of the law run the risk of becoming tainted by vestiges of Marcion's towering influence.

Jesus taught, "Think not that I have come to abolish the law and the prophets; I have come not to abolish but to fulfill" (Matt 5:17). Three words, "law," "abolish," and "fulfill," raise issues that are fundamental to New Testament theology. If Jesus fulfilled the law, then is it abolished? Some interpreters claim that Jesus is offering liberty from the yoke of the law because all has been fulfilled in his person. Although this approach tends to separate Christians from their biblical heritage, it finds strong support from certain sectors in the church. Laypeople and clergy who are untutored in the roots of Christian faith do not recognize that Marcion and his disciples taught a similar approach to the law and the prophets.

The church historian E. C. Blackman observed that Marcion and his disciples "undoubtedly adopted Mt. 5.17, after inverting the order of the clauses so as to give exactly an opposite sense."[7] According to their Bible, Jesus taught, "Think not that I have come to fulfill the law, I have not come to fulfill but to abolish . . ."[8] While few modern Christians would resort to changing the words of their Bible, they interpret the words of Jesus in a way that upholds their understanding of a sharp contrast between law and grace. Prejudiced exegesis can have the same result as altering the canonical text. Marcion's dualism taught that Jesus brought grace and abolished the Jewish law, which brought judgment. On the contrary, the Jewish understanding of Torah encompasses all that is known about God's grace. Divine grace is revealed in Torah. Torah and its deeper revelation of divine mercy and grace, however, are not always interpreted properly. As Christians, we must view the law through the eyes of Jesus.

Marcion certainly did not share Jesus' attitude toward the Judaism of his day. Neither did he share Paul's views, despite the fact that he claimed to be a disciple of Paul. Instead of seeing Torah and the prophets through the eyes of Jesus, Marcion sought to change the meaning of Jesus' teachings and to convert Paul's message into an anti-Jewish gospel. According to Epiphanius, Marcion taught "that Christ came down from above from the invisible and unnameable Father for the salvation of souls and the refutation of the God of the Jews, the law, the prophets, and suchlike."[9] He viewed Jesus and his teachings as revelation knowledge that abolished Judaism and the message of Torah for life. Was Marcion a genuine disciple of Paul? Did Marcion accurately represent Jesus' mission?

In the mind of Jesus, the Hebrew Bible taught God's love for all people and provided a practical guide for daily life. In light of Jesus' esteem for Torah, Matt 5:17 is certainly addressing the issue of properly comprehending the driving force behind the biblical text, which leads to right conduct. The Hebrew background of this verse clarifies its deeper meaning.[10] In rabbinic literature, the Greek words from the gospel that are translated "abolish" and "fulfill" possess dynamic equivalents. The word *abolish* means "interpret incorrectly." The Greek word *katalyō* means "abolish," and its dynamic Hebrew equivalent is *batel,* which also means "cancel, abolish, destroy." Often *batel* is used in contexts that deal with interpreting Scripture. A person cancels Torah when it is misunderstood.

How can one observe God's law if one does not comprehend what it requires? The word *fulfill,* moreover, refers to interpreting a passage accurately. The Hebrew equivalent of the Greek word *plēroō* is *kiyem.* The root of *kiyem* means "cause to stand" and has the sense of "uphold," "observe," "fulfill," or "place on a firmer footing." It too is used in contexts that deal with interpreting Scripture.[11] If one misunderstands the proper meaning of Torah, one may not obey the Lord's will and therefore will cancel the law. Hence, a person may abolish Torah by misconstruing the divine revelation. On the other hand, when one understands the proper meaning, one can obey God's will and therefore fulfill Torah. The theological polemics within Christianity during its struggle for self-definition caused the church to sever itself almost completely from Judaism. This created an environment in which Marcion's ideas could flourish. In its efforts to achieve self-definition, it was easy for the church to come under Marcion's anti-Judaism spell. Centuries later, during the Reformation period, many Protestant Reformers attacked the papacy. They wrongly used Torah and Judaism as the whipping boy for what they viewed as the incorrect teaching of the official church. Indeed, even today it is not unusual for Judaism to become the scapegoat for attacking all that is perceived as evil in the church's doctrine.[12] The good is seen as emanating from authentic Christianity, while the bad is portrayed wrongly as coming from Judaism.

As a result, the three key words of Matt 5:17, *law, abolish,* and *fulfill,* have assumed quite different meanings in their modern English translations from what they had in ancient Jewish thought. What did these three words mean to Jesus and his early followers? The Hebrew word *torah* is derived from the root *yarah,* which means "shoot an arrow" or "teach." Torah means teaching or instruction that is true and straight, as if the words of Torah are shot in a direct path like an arrow, with power and force for living life to the fullest. Torah is the divine aim for all people who love God. Torah means God's will, including, but going beyond, the ink dried upon the scrolls of holy writ. People, however, interpret the divine revelation of Torah in many different ways. Accurate interpretation breathes life and vitality into the words that were divinely spoken. If properly understood and obeyed, the divine revelation provides a guide for successful living. Thus the law is fulfilled. Wrong interpretation, on the other hand, cancels the words communicated through divine revelation. As Abraham Heschel has shown, while the Greeks studied to comprehend and Western thinkers study to apply their knowledge in a practical sense, the ancient Hebrews studied to revere.[13] Awe and reverence of God is the objective. God gave Torah. He is to be revered. Each human being stands in awe and wonder before God. The fear of God is foundational for true faith. Hence, the task of learning Torah is a sacred undertaking. Study leads to reverence. Reverence leads to obedience. Jesus came to accurately interpret Torah so that God, who gave it, will be revered and obeyed through proper action. *Abolish* means to obstruct through wrong interpretation. *Fulfill* refers to the proper understanding of the text, which leads to a lifestyle of holiness dedicated to God.

Paul's words in Romans drive home the same point. He does not contradict Jesus' saying. David Flusser has observed that Paul is very close to the spirit of Jesus' words in Matt 5:17 when the apostle declares, "Do we then overthrow the law by this faith? By no means! On the contrary, we uphold the law" (Rom 3:31).[14] The word *uphold* translates the Greek term *histēmi* "to stand," which in Hebrew is equivalent to *kiyem*, "cause to stand." The New English Bible better captures the essence of the idea by translating *histēmi* "to place on firmer footing." Paul is saying literally that his message strengthens the true meaning of Torah. Paul desired that the disciples of Jesus would become the servants of righteousness and live holy lives of true faith.[15]

Marcion, however, started with a "refutation of the God of the Jews." The very nature of God who is revealed in Torah is distorted in Marcion's anti-Judaism. He attacked the meaning of the Hebrew Scriptures and taught that they have no value or authority for the church. He interpreted Paul as teaching a new gospel that liberated people from the message of Torah so that they could rely on revelation knowledge. Marcion held that Jesus fulfilled his role as a divine revealer rather than as the expected Jewish Messiah. For Paul, however, Jesus fulfilled the mission of the Messiah. He was a historical figure who lived, taught, died, rose from the dead, and promised a future redemption. He was not a divine revealer who canceled the law. Paul's true message was subverted within Marcion's religious system, which espoused rebellion against the God of Israel.

Christianity's perspective of Torah plays a chief role in molding the church's doctrine of God. The divine nature is revealed in Torah. Marcion taught that the evil God of creation had given Torah. He is a God of legalism, who is contrasted with the God of light, whom people discover through revelation knowledge. Tertullian, an early church father, claimed that the heresy of Marcionism actually had compromised the divine nature. Marcion had departed from a proper understanding of God. By denying Torah, Marcion had denied God himself. Tertullian affirmed, "The Christian verity has distinctly declared this principle, 'God is not, if He is not one.'"[16] The belief in God's nature in Christian faith is rooted in Deut 6:4, "Hear O Israel, the LORD our God, the LORD is one," which was the essence of Judaism in the time of Jesus. Paul himself affirms, "God is one: and he will justify the circumcised on the ground of their faith and the uncircumcised through their faith" (Rom 3:30). In this verse, Paul stresses that "God is one." In reality, Marcion was attacking the doctrine of God when he declared that the Jewish Bible was defunct. The foundation of Christian belief is based upon the Jewish concept of God as revealed in Torah. Our perspective of Torah will determine our faith in God.

The difference between Jesus and Paul, on the one hand, and Marcion, on the other, may be summed up in one word—Torah. Paul warned Christians against arrogance. He knew that arrogant Christians would sever themselves from the root that nourished them.[17] Neither Jesus nor Paul were against Torah. They were not antinomians. Sadly, however, traditional Christian interpretations have been tainted by Marcion-like teachings that separate the message of Jesus from its rich Jewish heritage. Paul is described more as a Greek philosopher or Gnostic believer in Christian biographies than as a Pharisee or a Hebrew of the Hebrews, which is so crucial for his own autobiographical sketch. Jesus and Paul began with the Torah and did not depart from it. In reality, we as Christians, though grafted into the majestic olive tree, too often disconnect ourselves from its trunk and its life-giving roots.

JUDAISM AND CHRISTIANITY: DIVERSE PERSPECTIVES ON TORAH: NOTES

1. See J. Quasten, *Patrology* (4 vols.; Westminster, Md.: Christian Classics, 1986) 1.268–72. One of the finest treatments of Marcion remains Adolph von Harnack, *Marcion: Das Evangelium vom fremden Gott* (1924; reprint, Darmstadt: Wissenschaftliche Buchgesellschaft, 1985). More accessible to many readers is the short article of R. McL. Wilson, "Marcion," in *The Encyclopedia of Philosophy* (New York: Macmillan, 1972) 5.155f. Wilson correctly notes some of the distinctions between Marcion's theology and Gnosticism.

2. In the second stratum of Christianity, the issues of Christology became much more pivotal than the questions relating to Torah.

3. In *God in Search of Man,* 137, Heschel writes, "Faith comes out of awe, out of an awareness that we are exposed to His presence, out of anxiety to answer the challenge of God, out of an awareness of our being called upon. Religion consists of *God's question and man's answer.* The way *to* faith is the way *of* faith. The way to God is a way of God. Unless God asks the question, all our inquiries are in vain." Would the Apostle Paul disagree?

4. See Wilson, *Our Father Abraham,* 108ff.

5. See esp. P. Tomson, *Paul and the Jewish Law;* cf. C. Thoma, *A Christian Theology of Judaism* (Mahwah, N.J.: Paulist, 1980), with a long foreword by David Flusser.

6. On Matt 5:17–20, see esp. David Bivin and Roy Blizzard Jr., *Understanding the Difficult Words of Jesus* (Arcadia: Makor Foundation, 1983) 152–55. For a proper approach to the synoptic problem, see also the very important work of R. L. Lindsey, *A Hebrew Translation of the Gospel of Mark* (Jerusalem: Dugith Publishers, 1973). I have discussed the relationships between the Gospels in Young, *Jesus and His Jewish Parables,* 129–63.

7. E. C. Blackman, *Marcion and His Influence* (London: SPCK, 1948) 48.

8. Ibid.

9. P. Amidon, *The Panarion of St. Epiphanius* (New York: Oxford, 1990) 146. Sadly, for information about Marcion, the scholar must rely on what others wrote about him. Marcion's theology is known primarily from what Christian apologists said against his teachings.

10. One of the finest treatments of these issues relating to the Jewish concept of Torah appears in A. Heschel, *Torah min Hashamayim* (Hebrew; 3 vols.; London: Soncino, 1990). See also Heschel, *God in Search of Man,* 167ff.

11. See W. Bacher, *Die exegetische Terminologie der jüdischer Traditionslitera-tur* (reprint; Darmstadt, 1965).

12. This tendency is still prevalent in modern theology. Whatever is wrong with the church is conveniently traced back to Judaism or Pharisaism. Whatever is right is hailed as the innovation of Christianity. This simplistic approach to history and theology must be critically evaluated. Much of what is good in the church has its roots in Judaism. In fact, Paul's Pharisaism proved to be a treasure store for blossoming Christian theology. His doctrine of God and his teachings on the final redemption and the resurrection of the dead, e.g., flow from his Pharisaic roots. The Pharisees and the early Christians shared many common theological beliefs.

13. See Heschel, *God in Search of Man*, 3–2, 73–79, 43–53.

14. David Flusser, private communication to author. See Flusser, *Judaism and the Origins of Christianity*, 494–507.

15. See Rom 6, which is discussed in ch. 3 above. For a bibliography and further discussion, cf. also Dunn, *Romans*, 1.301–57.

16. Tertullian, *Against Marcion* 1.3, in A. Roberts and J. Donaldson, *The Ante-Nicene Fathers* (reprint; Peabody, Mass.: Hendrickson, 1994) 3.273. While Tertullian strongly attacks Marcion by citing the Christian truth of the nature of God, he is more ambivalent on the issue of Torah and is less than sympathetic toward the Jewish people in his other writings (cf. Tertullian, *An Answer to the Jews*, ibid., 3.152–73).

17. See Rom 9, 10, 11. See also the insights of Boers, "The Problem of Jews and Gentiles," 184–96.

5 The Torah: Roots of Grace and Faith in Paul's Message

The pattern is this: God has chosen Israel and Israel has accepted the election. In his role as King, God gave Israel commandments which they are to obey as best they can. Obedience is rewarded and disobedience punished. In case of failure to obey, however, man has recourse to divinely ordained means of atonement, in all of which repentance is required. As long as he maintains his desire to stay in the covenant, he has a share in God's covenantal promises, including life in the world to come. The intention and effort to be obedient constitute the condition for remaining in the covenant, but they do not earn it.

E. P. Sanders
Paul and Palestinian Judaism

CHRISTIAN thinking has a tendency to regard the law of the "old" covenant as irrelevant because of the grace of God that is revealed in the New Testament. Popular Christian theology, especially that of the dispensationalists, often seemingly maintains that the divine character was transformed from a God of legalism and law in the Old Testament into the God of grace and love in the New. The Old Testament is characterized as a book that endorses legalism in order to bring each individual to faith. Moreover, the Judaism of the time of Jesus is described as a works-righteousness religion, where every individual is required to earn his or her own salvation through personal merit and good deeds. This fundamental misunderstanding of early Jewish thought and the relationship between the Old Testament and the faith of the early church has so fouled the popular perception of Paul that to many what is true about Paul's opinion of the purpose of the law and of faith in Jesus sounds like heresy.

LAW AND GRACE IN THE BIBLE

The God of the Old Testament has not undergone a strange metamorphosis, like a schizophrenic patient revealing different patterns of behavior. We must recognize that the God of the Old Testament is the God of the New. He is described as being full of grace and mercy in *both* testaments. Even when Moses received the Torah on Mount Sinai, the Bible says, "The LORD passed before him, and proclaimed, 'The LORD, the LORD, a God merciful and gracious, slow to anger, and abounding in steadfast love . . .' " (Exod 34:6f.). Here in the heart of the law, on Mount Sinai itself, the Lord is described in terms of mercy and grace. Indeed, this is not the only place in the Hebrew Bible where mercy and grace are attributed to the Lord. The same description appears in many other Old Testament passages. Consider, for example, the words of Ps 103:8, "The LORD is merciful and gracious, slow to anger and abounding in steadfast love." The psalmist quite probably was hinting at Exod 34:6 because he knew that his hearers would be acquainted with this verse and the grace message flowing through the words of Torah. The Lord of Israel loves his people and shows them compassion. The Jewish mind-set of the Hebrew authors of the Bible was dominated by the concept of divine mercy.

While the grace of God is apparent in the Hebrew Scriptures, one cannot escape the New Testament warnings of future recompense and judgment. Just as the Old Testament is not exclusively a book of retribution and judgment, the New

Testament is not exclusively a book of mercy and grace. Numerous warnings of the coming wrath of God appear in the New Testament. Sometimes because of the way Christian teachers have spoken, we do not expect judgment for wrong in the New Testament, and grace in Torah. In the words of Jesus, however, there are more references to the fires of eternal punishment than in any other part of sacred Scripture. The book of Revelation describes the "lake of fire." This graphic image certainly presents a strong warning. The God who is described in both testaments is the Lord of creation to whom every human being owes obedience. Each individual is responsible to God for his or her actions. According to the Apostle Paul, every person must give an account before the judgment seat (Rom 14:10).

GRACE IN JUDAISM

Not only is the Old Testament deemed legalistic; so is the mainstream of Judaism from the time of Jesus. The misrepresentation of Torah as preaching a save-yourself-by-your-own-good-works gospel contributes to a completely distorted view of Jewish faith during the period of the New Testament. Late Second Temple Judaism, the Judaism during the time of Jesus, was not a salvation-by-works religion! Most Jewish teachers belonging to Pharisaic and later rabbinic Judaism emphasized God's goodness and willingness to accept all sinners who repent. After a careful and in-depth examination of Jewish thought from the period, E. P. Sanders concludes authoritatively:

> The theme of mercy—whether put in terms of God's mercy in electing Israel, God's mercy in accepting repentant sinners (repentance does not earn a reward, but is responded to by God in mercy), or God's "rewarding" the righteous because of his mercy—serves to assure that election and ultimately salvation

cannot be earned, but depend on God's grace. One can never be righteous enough to be worthy in God's sight of the ultimate gifts, which depend only on his mercy.[1]

The message of divine compassion is strong in the minds of the Jewish religious teachers from the time of the New Testament. Sanders makes it clear by his observation that "salvation cannot be earned, but depend[s] on God's grace."[2] Indeed, grace is a salient feature of Jewish theology. For instance, long before the birth of Jesus, the Jewish sage Joshua ben Sira exhorted his listeners with the message, "Or who ever called upon him and was overlooked? For the Lord is compassionate and merciful; he forgives sins and saves in time of affliction" (Sir 2:10–11). Ben Sira emphasizes divine mercy and God's willingness to forgive sins. The religious leaders of the Jewish people within the circles of the Pharisees—and their successors among the rabbis—pushed the message of grace beyond Old Testament borders. Like Jesus and Paul, they developed the concept of divine mercy.

GOD'S GRACE FOR SINNERS

A Jewish teacher who lived on the Israeli coast in the city of Caesarea, Rabbi Abbahu, emphasized the continuing Jewish tradition that God loves and receives sinners who repent. Like Joshua ben Sira from an earlier time, Rabbi Abbahu held that God is ready to receive repentant sinners and even gives them a position of preference:

> The place occupied by repentant sinners cannot be attained even by the completely righteous, for it is written, "Peace, peace, to him that is far off, and to him that is near" (Isaiah 57:19), thus, first he that is "far off," then he that is "near."[3]

The rabbis, and the sages who preceded them, further cultivated the Old Testament idea of mercy and emphasized divine compassion. Indeed, the rabbis believed that a person could attain the future life in a moment of true repentance. God's mercy will be given to the sinner.

When we Christians misconstrue these elements of Jewish theology from both the Old Testament and Second Temple Judaism, we fail to grasp Paul's intent. What did Paul want? Did he desire to repudiate the law? Whom was he confronting with his argument of righteousness through faith in Christ? In this brief discussion it is impossible to deal adequately with all the problems surrounding these issues, but we will examine Paul's words in Romans and Galatians in order to shed light upon these penetrating questions.

As a start, it is helpful to observe Luke's description of the crisis that Paul, Barnabas, and later the members of the Jerusalem council addressed when a group of teachers from Judea began preaching to the non-Jews that without circumcision there is no salvation: "Unless you are circumcised according to the custom of Moses, you cannot be saved" (Acts 15:1). Is circumcision a prerequisite of salvation for the Gentiles? This pressing question, which was legal or halakic in nature, dominated the discussion of the relationship between Jews and non-Jews in the community of faith.[4] Should the Gentiles convert to Judaism before they are accepted as followers of Jesus and received into the congregation?

Concerning the issue of salvation, Paul was adamant that the observance of the law was not the means by which the individual could become righteous. The redemptive act of Jesus' suffering provides the way of salvation. But does this mean that the law serves no good purpose? Paul maintained that Torah provides an indispensable guide for a moral life that Christians must follow. One is not saved by observance of the law, and non-Jews are not required to convert to Judaism in order to be good Christians. In Jewish thought, all of the commandments of Torah are required of Israel, but the Gentiles are responsible only for its moral demands, which are epitomized in the covenant with Noah and his children. This is basically the position endorsed by the Jerusalem council (Acts 15:28–29).[5] Gentiles who have accepted the message of Jesus and want to join the fellowship of the community will be responsible for the moral standard outlined in the Noachic covenant, but they do not have to be circumcised and assume Israel's entire covenantal responsibilities.[6]

WORKS OF THE FLESH

But does this mean that believers should continue in sin in order to enjoy the overabundance of God's grace? Paul replies with an emphatic "no" (Rom 6:1). The law is good (Rom 7:12). The problem is that people have difficulty obeying it. Jesus did not cancel the law, and the preaching of faith does not destroy its message (Rom 3:31). Should murders and adulteries be permitted in a mind-set opposed to Torah? Is that what Paul means by freedom from the law? By no means: Paul demanded a high moral standard of all his congregations. Even in Galatians, he solemnly warns,

> Do not use your freedom as an opportunity for the flesh. . . . Now the works of the flesh are plain: immorality, impurity, licentiousness, idolatry, sorcery, enmity, strife, jealousy, anger, selfishness, dissension, party spirit, envy, drunkenness, carousing, and the like. I warn you, as I warned you before, that those who do such things shall not inherit the kingdom of God.[7]

Like other Jewish teachers, Paul desired conduct in harmony with the law. Paul, the Jewish apostle to the Gentiles, teaches, "The commandments, 'You shall not commit adultery, You shall not kill, You shall not steal, You shall not covet,' and any other commandment, are summed up in this sentence, 'You shall love your neighbor as yourself.' "[8] Similar summaries of the law are attributed to the eminent teacher Hillel as well as to the famous Rabbi Akiva.[9] Rabban Gamaliel, the grandson of Hillel, would have filled his pupil Paul with the teachings of Judaism. This law of love from Lev 19:18 was considered a summary of the whole Torah. It embodied all the commandments. If one upholds this command, one will observe the rest.

FAITH'S REWARDS

Paul teaches that faith enables a person to attain the righteousness of God and that there is no tension between it and the law. The term *faith* is better understood in certain contexts as "faithfulness," because the concept includes so much more than the English words *belief* or *trust*. Righteousness involves the redemptive work of God in the salvation process and in the renewed lives of the faithful. It is so much more dynamic and forceful than the motionless idea that one is declared righteous at a fixed time. Righteousness is rooted in Torah. It is active and powerful to bring about a transformation of conduct. For Paul, faith, righteousness, and Torah go together. With what seems to be great enthusiasm, he argues, "Do we then overthrow the law by this faith? By no means! On the contrary, we uphold the law" (Rom 3:31). After stating his case firmly, Paul launches into a deep discussion about the righteousness of Abraham, which is based upon faith (Rom 4). Paul's interpretation of Gen 15:6, "Abraham believed God and it was accounted to him as righteousness," is in the form of a Jewish midrash, a distinct type of commentary on Scripture. Paul uses midrash here in order to penetrate the deeper meaning of righteousness in the Scripture. Paul is not alone in interpreting righteousness with this sense.

The famous Jewish interpreter Rashi also understood the expression "righteousness" to denote merit or benefit. In the *Mekilta*, an early midrashic commentary on the book of Exodus, we discover that Abraham's faith possessed great significance for the rabbis. When dealing with the verse "they [the people of Israel] believed in the LORD and in his servant Moses" (Exod 14:31), the rabbis extol the importance of vibrant faith:

> Great indeed is faith before Him who spoke and the world came into being. For as a reward for the faith with which Israel believed in God the Holy Spirit rested upon them. . . . And so also you find that our father Abraham inherited both this world and the world beyond only as a reward for the faith with which he believed, as it is said: "And he believed in the Lord," etc. (Gen. 15:6).[10]

The merit of the fathers is a powerful concept in Jewish thought. Here the concept of the merit of the fathers is connected to faith and righteousness. In many ways, it is the example of the fathers that shows others the path to follow. The rabbis viewed Abraham's faith as his benefit and his future reward. His faith in God produced obedience. Abraham actively believed the Lord and followed him. It was credited to him as righteousness. Like the rabbis, Paul employed a similar motif when he preached about Abraham's faith as producing divine favor.

FAITH AND RIGHTEOUSNESS IN THE DEAD SEA SCROLLS

A latent reference to this understanding of righteousness also appears in the Dead Sea Scrolls. The meaning of the scroll *Miqsat Maaseh Torah,* "A Summary of the Precepts of the Torah," will continue to be debated by scholars in the future. It seems to be an epistle from the Dead Sea community to the leader of the Pharisees. The Pharisees, or whoever received the epistle, are urged to accept the words of the letter in good faith in order that "it would be counted to them as righteousness."[11]

Remember David, who was a man of mercy and who was delivered from many troubles and was forgiven. Hence, we write to you a summary of the works of Torah that we consider for your well-being and for your people because we have seen your people's cunning and knowledge of Torah. Understand all these matters. Ask him to enable you to correct your counsel and to remove from yourself evil thoughts and the counsel of Belial in order that you may rejoice in the end time by your finding correctness in the summary of our words; and it will be accounted unto you as righteousness in your doing what is right and good before him for your well-being and for all Israel.[12]

The epistle from the Dead Sea Scrolls calls its readers to accept the teachings of the Jewish sect in the wilderness of Judea. If the initial suggestions of the editors of the epistle are correct, the Pharisees are being asked to receive the truth of the Dead Sea community's teachings. When they accept the proper approach to life by embracing the contents of the epistle, then the righteousness of God will be given to them. The concept of righteousness is linked to salvation and redemption in the end time. The terminology of the sect is striking and very similar to Paul's discussion in Romans and Galatians.[13]

FAITH IN THE TEACHER OF RIGHTEOUSNESS

In another passage from the Dead Sea Scrolls, the community's Bible commentators interpret God's famous answer to the prophet Habakkuk, "but the righteous shall live by his faith" (Hab 2:4). Their comment on this verse depicts the members of the congregation in terms of their faith in the Teacher of Righteousness and efforts to be obedient to his instruction. They will be saved by faith.[14] But their faith is accompanied by works.

"[But the righteous will live by his faith]" (Hab 2:4): Its interpretation refers to all those who observe Torah in the House of Judah.

God will deliver them from the House of Judgment because of their work and because of their faith in the Teacher of Righteousness.[15]

Faith and works are fused together in this interpretation of Hab 2:4. (*Miqsat Maaseh Torah* also joins faith and righteousness, alluding to Gen 15:6, "Abraham believed God and it was accounted unto him as righteousness.") The commentary on Hab 2:4 focuses on believing the message of the Teacher of Righteousness and faithfully following his teachings with action. The members of the Dead Sea Community will be saved from the house of judgment in the end times because of their faith and corresponding actions. Paul's method of Bible interpretation is similar to the commentaries discovered among the Dead Sea Scrolls at Qumran.[16] One thing is certain: the Dead Sea community believed that faith, works of Torah, and having righteousness accounted to the believer all fit together in their understanding of the divine purpose. Works of Torah are not viewed as antagonistic to faith. Faith and works are inseparable. In a similar way, Paul urges his hearers to respond in faith like that of Abraham, who pioneered the way to righteousness. Pauline theology thus closely parallels Jewish thought from the first century.

PAUL AND HIS INTERPRETERS

The tremendous challenge for us today is to read Paul's letters without being influenced by the multiplicity of opinions of learned men in the past. First and foremost among such men is Martin Luther.[17] He, more than any other interpreter, has erected a stained-glass window through which we view Paul and his message. Instead of viewing Paul against the background of first-century Judaism, we see him through the eyes of later interpreters who knew little about early Jewish thought. Even today Luther's ideas about Paul continue to circulate widely in Protestant theological discussion. Certainly Luther's influence reaches beyond his time and place in history. But Paul's concerns about Jews and non-Jews living together in the community of faith did not trouble Luther. He faced radically different challenges and set other priorities.

Interpreters of Paul must ask the questions that Paul asked before they apply his answers to their own problems, or else they may find themselves coupling Paul's answers with the wrong set of questions. Luther developed an ambivalent attitude to the law because of his own struggles, which were essentially foreign to New Testament Christianity. For instance, his stance on the epistle of James implied that Torah canceled faith. He also leaned too far in the opposite direction, suggesting that genuine faith canceled Torah. In the end, had Luther had his way, he probably would have opted to drop from the New Testament these five troublesome chapters penned by Jesus' brother James. So uncritical acceptance of Luther's interpretation ultimately leads to questioning the content of the canon itself. While Luther made significant positive contributions to Christian theology, helping many to understand divine grace and human need, his approach to faith and works was radically influenced by his own time. Students of Pauline literature must comprehend first-century Judaism apart from later church controversies.

Krister Stendahl has noted the prominence of these teachings in church tradition:

> Especially in the Protestant tradition—and particularly among Lutherans—it is Paul's Epistle to the Romans which holds a position of honor, supplying patterns of thought that are lifted into the position of overarching and organizing principles for Pauline material. Paul's presentation of justification by faith . . . was hammered out by Paul for the very specific and limited purpose of defending the rights of Gentile converts to be full and genuine heirs to the promises of God to Israel. Their rights were

based solely on faith in Jesus Christ. This was Paul's very special stance, and he defended it zealously against any compromise . . .[18]

Students of Paul must seek to understand the first-century social and religious issues that divided the early Christians. For Paul, justification by faith united Jews and Gentiles in a rich cultural diversity that paved the way for a righteous lifestyle.

Other famous scholarly critics, such as F. C. Baur, have argued that the New Testament developed as a series of debates surrounding a thesis and a corresponding antithesis. Paul's thesis, "salvation through faith without works," was answered by James with the antithesis, "Faith without works is dead." In reality, Paul believed that the fruit of the faith would produce a holy lifestyle. He was very much aware of the activity of the Holy Spirit in the life of the individual. On the other hand, although James never denied the value of faith and he esteemed faith in the life of the believer, he emphasized that true faith always produces corresponding actions. Faith without works is no faith.

Perhaps the origin of these deficient scholarly approaches to the beginnings of Christianity is rooted in a misunderstanding of Judaism during the time of Jesus. Did Luther understand Paul and his context properly? Has F. C. Baur understood the relationship between Paul and James? Paul's message must be interpreted in its context of a mixed community, comprising Jews and Gentiles, united in their embracing of faith in the one God of Israel and his Messiah, Jesus of Nazareth. Faith leads to righteousness—in other words, a righteous way of living that is pleasing to God.

In large measure, Paul's use of the word *righteousness* is the source of the differing interpretations. Luther understood it in the sense of the German word *Gerechtigkeit,* meaning "justification," or a position of right standing before God. I believe that this interpretation does not adequately deal with Paul's

employment of the term in numerous contexts. In fact, Paul
would feel that he has been grossly misunderstood if the
righteousness of God is interpreted to mean only a state of
justification. Paul's problem was a believer's problem. How is
it possible to experience God's redemption in everyday life?
Paul clearly states that the believer is to become a "slave of
righteousness" for obedience (Rom 6:17). When the force of
Paul's message is grasped, Luther's views become unsatisfac-
tory. His concept is too static. Righteousness is so much more
than a state of justification. The life of righteousness is a
dynamic experience! It is the power of God to live righteous
lives of obedience. This is true redemption and salvation because it embraces the new life of following Jesus. As a path to
salvation, the way of righteousness is experienced as a present
reality that culminates in the Parousia. A supernatural strength
enables the believer to participate in the redemptive movement—the kingdom of God (Gal 5:21). For Paul, God's power
is released through faith in Jesus.

PAUL'S CULTURE AND FAITH EXPERIENCE

The most effective way to correct these misleading interpretations is to translate the scriptures with a sensitivity to
Paul's cultural context. The problem of understanding Paul's
use of the term *righteousness* is indeed a complex and a difficult issue of exegesis. In light of the above facts, the term
would often be better translated "life of righteousness" or
"way of righteous living" rather than with the standard meaning of a state of justification. In Paul's faith experience, he
walked in the way of righteousness, as he believed in Jesus and
received empowerment from the Holy Spirit. The "life of
righteousness" or "way of righteous living" means salvation or
true redemption. It culminates in God's final judgment. This
life is the preparation for the eschaton. The disciple becomes
involved in the redemptive actions of helping others as a

consequence of his or her relationship with God through faith in Jesus. The hungry need food; the destitute, clothing; the homeless, shelter; the sick and those in prison, personal attention. The follower of Jesus must pursue purposeful acts of redemption—living a life of selfless service for suffering humanity. For Paul, the way of righteousness is indeed God's highest salvation, because it is the liberation of the flesh into the life of the Spirit; and that holy life is characterized by joining with God in his redemptive outreach to a hurting world.

In the final analysis, the conceptual values of grace and faith in Paul's teachings are riveted in Torah. Faith leads to righteousness. Grace opens the door for the individual to experience God in the dynamics of everyday life. Paul boldly proclaims, "But now that you have been set free from sin and have become slaves of God, the return you get is sanctification and its end, eternal life. For the wages of sin is death, but the gift of God is eternal life in Christ Jesus our Lord" (Rom 6:22–23).

THE TORAH ROOTS OF GRACE AND FAITH IN PAUL'S MESSAGE: NOTES

1. Sanders, *Paul and Palestinian Judaism*, 421–22.

2. Ibid., 422. See also the note on ʾ*Abot* 2:7 in Hertz, *The Authorized Daily Prayer Book*, 634. On the saying of Hillel, which teaches reward and punishment, Hertz observes, "Repentance alone, they [the rabbis] held, could counter-act the operation of this rule. 'There are those who acquire eternal life in years upon years; there are those who (by repentance) acquire it in an hour,' said Rabbi Judah the Prince."

3. See Rabbi Abbahu, *b. Ber.* 34b.

4. See Stendahl, *Paul Among Jews and Gentiles.*

5. Acts 15 explains that the Gentiles will be held responsible for select laws that seem to be an early summary of the commandments for the children of Noah (Acts 15:19–21, 29; 21:25; see *b. Sanh.* 56a and parallels; and cf. *Jub.* 7). These moral principles were thought to be universal, while Torah

was the treasured gift from God to Israel. The covenant with Israel could not be broken. But the laws for the non-Jews focus on the decisive break they have made with their former idolatrous practices, on a firm belief in the one true God, and on basic teachings for a moral way of life. For Paul, these guidelines for a moral lifestyle were a natural result of the empowerment of the Holy Spirit (see Gal 5). He highly valued holiness. For a fine treatment of the issues surrounding the council in Jerusalem, see Flusser, "Paul's Jewish-Christian Opponents in the Didache"; and also esp. Flusser and Safrai, "Das Aposteldekret und die Noachitischen Gebote."

6. Ibid.

7. See Gal 5:13–21. In reality, Paul's view of the life in the Spirit went beyond the basic principles of conduct outlined in Acts 15. Paul viewed the relationship of Israel to God as permanent, and he highly valued the special identity God had given solely to the Jewish people. The Gentiles who became Christians must live holy lives according to the power of the Holy Spirit.

8. Rom 12:9f.; see Gal 5:14. The great importance Paul placed upon Torah and its proper interpretation has seldom been appreciated by scholars. For a new approach that recognizes Paul's understanding of halakah, midrash, and its application in the practical life of the church, see Tomson, *Paul and the Jewish Law.*

9. See *b. Šabb.* 31a; *Avot de Rabbi Natan,* version B, ch. 26; cf. Tob 4:14. See also the note on *ʾAbot* 2:21 by Hertz, *Authorized Daily Prayer Book,* 644–46.

10. See *Mekilta de Rabbi Ishmael* on Exod 14:31, in the Hebrew edition of H. S. Horovitz, *Mekhilta* (Jerusalem: Wahrmann Books, 1970) 114.

11. See Elisha Qimron and John Strugnell, *Qumran Cave 4: Miqsat Maʿase ha-Torah* (Oxford: Clarendon, 1994) 61–63; and "An Unpublished Halakhic Letter from Qumran," *Israel Museum Journal* (Spring 1985) 9–12 and in *Biblical Archaeology Today* (Jerusalem, 1985) 400–407. On *Miqsat Maaseh Torah,* cf. also Yaakov Sussmann, "The History of Halakah and the Dead Sea Scrolls—a Preliminary to the Publication of 4QMMT," *Tarbitz* 59 (1990) 11–76 (Hebrew); and David Flusser, "Some of the Precepts of the Torah from Qumran (4QMMT) and the Benediction against the Heretics," *Tarbitz* 61 (1992) 333–74.

12. The Hebrew text was also printed in Flusser, *Judaism and the Origins of Christianity,* 722. Here I offer a provisional English translation.

13. See also Flusser, "The Dead Sea Sect." Flusser discusses the close relationship between Paul and the thought of the Essenes who wrote the Dead Sea Scrolls.

14. On the scroll's reference to "their faith in the Teacher of Righteousness," A. Dupont-Sommer, *The Essene Writings from Qumran* (Gloucester, Mass.: Peter Smith, 1973) 263 n. 4, observes, "The Teacher of Righteousness tries the hearts of men; it is faith in him that saves."

15. 1QpHab. 8:1 (author's translation). The best edition of the text is Bilha Nitzan, *Pesher Habakkuk: A Scroll from the Wilderness of Judaea (1QpHab)* (Jerusalem: Bialik Institute, 1986) 175. For other English translations, see T. Gaster, *The Dead Sea Scriptures* (3d ed.; Garden City, N.J.: Anchor, 1976) 322; and G. Vermes, *The Dead Sea Scrolls in English* (3d ed.; New York: Penguin, 1988) 287. Nitzan observes that the phrase "those who observe the Torah," in 1QpHab 2:4, describes the members of the community who live according to the sect's way of life in its own interpretation of the Jewish law's halakic requirements (p. 175).

16. The importance of this Qumran text (1QpHab. 8:1) and its relationship to the halakic letter from Qumran and to Paul were discussed by Tomson, *Paul and the Jewish Law*, 66. Tomson has observed the continuity between Paul, the Dead Sea sect, and the rabbis in their treatments of the issue of faith, works, and righteousness.

17. Cf. the discussion and bibliographical materials presented in John Reumann, *Righteousness in the New Testament* (Mahwah, N.J.: Paulist, 1982). This work resulted in part from dialogue and reflection between Lutheran and Roman Catholic biblical scholars. Especially insightful and sensitive is the response by Joseph Fitzmyer at the conclusion of the book.

18. Stendahl, *Paul Among Jews and Gentiles*, 1–2.

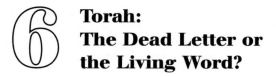

Torah:
The Dead Letter or
the Living Word?

But Paul's pre-eminent contribution to the world has
been his presentation of the good news of free grace—as he
himself would have put it (rightly), his re-presentation of
the good news explicit in Jesus' teaching and embodied in
his life and work.

F. F. Bruce
Paul: Apostle of the Heart Set Free

Is Paul against the law? Is Torah to be viewed like a dead husband whom nobody really liked? This is the way some Christians have interpreted Rom 7:1–6. Paul makes an apology:

> For the woman who has a husband is bound by the law to her husband as long as he lives. But if the husband dies she is released from the law of her husband. (v. 2)

Commonly the illustration is read as if Torah is analogous to a dead husband. The apostle is not suggesting that like a woman freed from an unpleasant husband, we are now liberated to do what we please; rather, using a point of ancient Jewish law, Paul illustrates his relationship with Torah in light of his new faith in Jesus. He is reaching deep into his Jewish heritage in order to find a metaphor to help explain the impact faith in Jesus has had on his understanding of Torah and the sinfulness of the human condition. As a Jewish theologian, however, the influence of Torah permeates his thinking. For Paul, Torah is good. It is the living word of God that is sacred. When the flesh dies, the believer is free to obey Torah in the new life of the Spirit. The human condition, however, drives each person into the bondage of sin.

Paul's approach underscores the necessity for Christians to have a proper view toward Judaism and its teachings. Without such a view, Christians forfeit the ability to penetrate Paul's message. The background imagery flows from ancient Judaism. Paul indeed mentions the death of a husband. But could Paul be using this as a metaphor for the death of the flesh? Have we misconstrued the message of Paul? Is Torah for Paul really a deceased husband? I believe that Paul was speaking about dying to the sinfulness of the flesh rather than to the sacredness of Torah.

As Christians, we should take the study of Torah and Jewish approaches to the Bible very seriously.[1] Paul certainly did. At times, he was nearly consumed with the issues surrounding faith in Jesus and Torah as they related to his missionary work as a Jewish apostle sent to the Gentiles. Sadly, we seldom recognize that much of what Paul says about Torah must be interpreted in the context of his understanding of Jews and Gentiles, with their respective distinctions, as equal partners in God's family.[2] The Greek text of Rom 10:4, moreover, as mentioned above in chapter 2, is mistranslated sometimes to read, "For Christ is the end of the law . . ." It should read, "For Messiah [i.e., Christ] is the aim [or goal] of Torah [law] . . ."[3] How else can one read Paul's strong affirmation in Rom 3:31, "Do we then make void the law [Torah] through faith? Certainly not! On the contrary we establish the law [Torah]." Either Paul is theologically schizophrenic or some of his interpreters have neglected key aspects of his thought.

Here we seek to establish the background of Rom 7:1–6 in order to view Paul's approach to the law, the flesh, and the analogy of the "dead husband" within the framework of first-century Jewish thought. To interpret Paul correctly on this passage, it is first imperative to recognize that the saying "When a person dies, he is free from the law and the commandments" *(kivan shemet adam naaseh chofshi men hatorah vehamitzvot)* was a well-known legal or halakic concept that probably was almost proverbial in ancient Jewish thought.[4] When Paul says that he is writing to those who know the law (Rom 7:1), he is obviously speaking about a practice of halakah, with which the Jews in the congregation of Rome would be quite familiar. The marriage laws concerning man and wife were fairly well known among the Jewish people. Rabban Gamaliel the Elder, who according to Luke was the teacher of Paul in his early days as a student in Jerusalem, addressed questions relating to these laws in the Mishnah. Gamaliel taught that a woman is free to remarry even if only one witness gives testimony that her husband had died (*m. Yebam.* 16:7).[5] Scholars have noted that the passage in Rom 7:1–6 might well betray the influence of Paul's teacher Gamaliel.[6] While the similarity between Paul and Gamaliel on this point of halakah should not be denied, it is also true that such teachings were probably common knowledge, widespread among Jewish men and women who lived pious lives according to their faith. Paul could have been acquainted with this principle from many sources. One may have been Gamaliel the Elder. Indeed, it was because this principle was so well known that Paul employed the halakah to make his point.

A SLAVE TO SIN OR GOD

The problem facing us is that many Christian interpreters, probably quite unintentionally, destroy Paul's message by saying—in so many words—that since Paul died to Torah, he is free to do whatever he pleases. According to this interpretation, Christians are free to pursue whatever sort of lifestyle they desire because they are, after all, free from the bondage of the law. They are not bound morally and ethically. But does this radical approach make sense in light of Romans 6? There Paul speaks about slavery to the flesh, which forces a person to disobey God. The apostle desires obedience to God and a dedication to righteousness. Piety characterizes Paul's own life. The Holy Spirit enables the apostle to live a life of service to God. In Rom 7:1–6, he employs an analogy based upon Jewish law. It stands to reason that Jewish sources can throw additional light upon Paul's message and the conclusion he desires to draw from the evidence he cites. The rabbis also discussed the problem of fleshly desires, which they commonly referred to as the "evil inclination." They were aware that the power of the evil inclination can place a person into bondage. Each person, however, should seek to serve the true Master who created him or her rather than the inclination to disobey God. In his teachings, the sage Rabbi Simeon ben Pazzi uses many of the same images as are found in Paul's writings. Here Rabbi Simeon ben Pazzi teaches about being "a slave to sin or God":

> "and the servant is free from his master" (Job 3:19). A person, as long as he lives is a servant to two masters: the servant of his Creator and of his [evil] inclination.[7] When he does the will of his Creator, he angers his inclination, and when he does the will of his inclination, he angers his Creator. When he dies, he is freed, "the servant is free from his master!"[8]

Rabbi Simeon ben Pazzi's saying "When he dies, he is freed . . ." not only recalls Paul's words in Rom 7:1–6 but also provides a clear parallel in thought to Paul's discussion of the servant who is enslaved either to his evil inclination or to his Creator. In Romans 6, Paul teaches that an individual is either a servant of sin to obey the flesh or a servant of righteousness to obey God.

David Flusser and Shmuel Safrai have commented upon the teaching of Rabbi Simeon ben Pazzi with regard to Jesus' teaching about serving one of two masters—money or God. One point of their discussion is pertinent for our purpose. They observe, "According to Rabbi Shimeon ben Pazzi, man, while he is alive, is the slave of his inclination, but after his death, his only master is God."[9] This perspective also has a direct bearing upon Paul and his analogy of marriage. Did Paul desire to abolish the law by saying that a person has died spiritually through faith in Jesus? Comparative study with rabbinic sources undermines this facile conclusion. What Paul is trying to say is that a person dies to his or her evil inclination, in order that he or she may become a servant of God alone. The sinful flesh dies so that the person may become a servant of righteousness (see Rom 6). Hence the individual is free to live a life pleasing to God.

Paul maintained a high standard of morality and ethics. When he wrote his epistle to the Galatians, for instance, he spelled out the works of the flesh as well as the fruit of the Spirit (see Gal 5:13–25). He also maintained that if one is circumcised, he is required to keep all the law; that is, not only the moral laws applicable to the children of Noah, but also all the commandments of the covenant made at Sinai with the children of Israel (Gal 5:3). According to Luke, Paul had Timothy circumcised (Acts 16:1–3). Paul's teachings and actions do not suggest that he viewed Torah as a legalistic system that is opposed to grace. The law is imbued with God's grace and his divine compassion. An individual is not saved from eternal punishment by meticulously keeping the law but by God's grace alone. This, however, is not to say that faith without corresponding actions has value. Although one can never earn the salvation of one's soul by observing Torah, even for Paul, faith without works has no meaning. Through grace the believer is given the power to live a holy life pleasing to God and thus to fulfill Torah (see Rom 3:31).

The point Paul was making in the marriage analogy of Rom 7:1–6 is simple. The individual dies to his flesh. The sinful flesh dies in order that the person may live and serve God alone. Paul would sharply disagree with Christian interpreters who claim that because one has died in Jesus, the teaching of Torah is void. Paul is not against Torah. Torah should not be identified with sin. Paul himself explicitly cautions his readers by declaring, "What shall we say then? Is the law sin? Certainly not!" (Rom 7:7). Rather, Paul affirms that Torah is spiritual (Rom 7:14, 8:3). It is holy and good (Rom 7:12). It is a custodian that leads the believer to Jesus by demonstrating the individual's need for spiritual power and salvation through faith.

Torah is neither the problem nor its solution. The problem is sin. The conflict between law and sin also appears in ancient Jewish sources. Second Esdras, a Jewish text written not long after the destruction of the temple in 70 CE, affirms the everlasting nature of Torah in spite of human sin: "For we who have received the law and sinned will perish, as well as our heart which received it; the law, however, does not perish but remains in its glory" (2 Esd 9:36–37). The parallels to Pauline theology in this text are remarkable. Paul's concern for sin is deeply embedded in his Jewish background. Sin does not cancel the law. Torah reveals the sin by exposing human unrighteousness in light of divine holiness. It reveals both the sacred and the profane.

Paul's love for Torah was not diminished by his encounter with Jesus. His approach to Rom 7:1–6 demonstrates the apostle's belief in the validity of the halakah and his faithfulness to his religious heritage. Furthermore, for Paul, Torah spoke of the mission of Jesus. Paul's entire worldview, Torah-centered, absorbed a fresh awakening concerning God's redemptive purpose. The teachings of Jesus, his life, death, and resurrection, followed by the empowerment of the Spirit, compelled Paul to integrate his revolutionary insight into all that he understood about the divine strategy for welcoming the Gentiles into God's family. His theology focuses upon Jesus at the center as revealed in Torah and reaches out for a life of righteousness as its aim. This Jesus-centered life, this life of righteousness, must be characterized by a proper understanding of the divine will as expressed in Torah. Jesus is the purpose of Torah that the Christian fulfills by faith. As the apostle to the Gentiles, Paul realized that Jesus is the reason for the spreading of faith in Israel's one God throughout the pagan world. Moreover, bringing the pagan peoples to faith is among the highest objectives of God's redemptive activity.

Torah, then, is not evil. On the contrary, Torah is spiritual and good, revealing the divine plan for all peoples. Through Paul's eyes, Jesus is revealed in Torah. The power of sin is undermined through the death and resurrection of Jesus. Long before Paul, the Pharisees already had stressed the doctrine of the resurrection. Here Paul's Pharisaic roots emerge as he struggles with the issue of the power of sin in a person's life. He strived for religious piety through a vibrant personal relationship with God through faith in Jesus the Messiah. Not Torah, but the individual's response to the divine revelation in God's law, is the problem. Torah reveals the sinfulness of humankind. But each person is free to respond negatively or positively to the message of Torah. It is the individual's response that determines whether Torah is the "law of sin and death" or the "Spirit of life in Christ Jesus" (Rom 8:2). The power of the resurrection impacts the believer's life. Through the Holy Spirit's empowerment, the Christian is able to live a holy life pleasing to God, thus fulfilling the requirements of Torah in the reality of personal experience.

In summation, Paul did not compare Torah to a corpse. On the contrary, he used a well-known legal principle to illustrate the deeper meaning of Torah. Employing metaphoric language, Paul speaks of the death to the flesh that becomes the seed of the resurrection life. The apostle declares, "For he who has died is freed from sin" (Rom 6:7). Through death to self, one is able to walk in the new life of the Spirit. When the flesh dies, one stops trying to obey God through one's own power. An individual relies, rather, upon the power of God, demonstrated in the resurrection of the Messiah, to provide strength. Through Jesus, according to Pauline theology, the individual is able to live for God by dying to the sinful flesh, thus serving the divine purpose in newness of life. So for Paul, Torah is not a dead letter, but the living word strengthened through Jesus and the power of the Holy Spirit living inside the believer.

TORAH: THE DEAD LETTER OR THE LIVING WORD? NOTES

1. Certainly Jesus himself treated the law with extreme care. See Young, *Jesus and His Jewish Parables*; and David Flusser, *Judaism and the Origins of Christianity.*

2. See Stendahl, *Paul Among Jews and Gentiles.*

3. It is beyond our study here to discuss this in full. See Howard, "Christ the End of the Law."

4. See not only *b. Nid.* 61b but also *b. Šabb.* 30a, 151b; *b. Pesah* 51b; *j. Kil.* 32a, ch. 9, hal. 4; cf. also *m. Qidd.* 1:1; and Urbach, *The Sages,* 1.379. I have greatly benefited from S. Safrai and D. Flusser, "The Slave of Two Masters," *Immanuel* 6 (1976) 30–33. Though Safrai and Flusser do not discuss Rom 7, their analysis of the rabbinic texts and the manuscript readings of the literature is of inestimable value. The sayings of Jesus concerning the two masters will not be understood without consideration of this article and its treatment of the Dead Sea Scrolls and the rabbinic literature.

5. The discussion deals with the case of an *agunah* (a deserted, literally a "tied" wife), i.e., a woman whose husband has disappeared without giving her a writ of divorce. Her husband may have died during a journey, while at war, or in some other such situation where his death must be confirmed by witnesses. She is free from the marriage contract only through divorce or through the death of her husband. After his death is documented, she is allowed to remarry. Rabban Gamaliel eased the law for women by his halakic ruling.

6. On this text and other possible allusions to Paul's knowledge of Gamaliel's teachings, see the critical discussion and analysis of Schoeps, *Paul,* 37 n. 3.

7. Here the Hebrew text has a play on words between *yetzer* (inclination) and *yotzer* (Creator). I have inserted the word *evil* to make the passage clear. Many scholars see a close similarity between the Pauline usage of "flesh" and the rabbinic term "evil inclination." The text in *Ruth Rabbah* deals with the spiritual battle between God's will and human desires contrary to the divine purpose.

8. The best edition of *Ruth Rabbah* is M. Lerner, "Midrash Ruth Rabbah" (Ph.D. diss., Hebrew University, 1971) 78–80. See also the commentary to the text, 24. Cf. the Vilna edition, Ruth Rabbah 3:1, 6a. See also the English translation of L. Rabinowitz, *Midrash Rabbah Ruth* (London: Soncino, 1983) 8.41.

9. See Safrai and Flusser, "The Slave of Two Masters," 31. See n. 4, above.

The Transcendence of Torah in Paul's Teachings

These Jews should be treated with sharp mercy, their synagogues set on fire with sulfur and pitch thrown in, their houses destroyed. They are to be herded together in stables. . . . Their prayer books, their Talmud, and their Bibles are to be taken from them. Their rabbis are to be forbidden on pain of death to give instructions, to praise God in public, and to pray to him. . . . Their money and jewelry, gold and silver, are to be taken from them since everything they possess has been stolen through usury.[1]

Martin Luther

IN Paul's teachings, Torah possesses a transcendence that goes beyond systematic theology or rigid dogma. Paul's view of Torah is not unlike that of other Jewish thinkers in the first century. But it is very unlike that of Marcion, who, as we have seen, became the leader of an influential movement that viewed Torah as the dark teachings of the Creator God.[2] Marcion maintained that the legalism of the Hebrew Bible had been fulfilled and a new dispensation of grace had been inaugurated. In ancient Jewish thought, Torah was viewed as a powerful force of goodness. In Judaism, Torah was compared to light. In Paul's teachings, Torah possesses a mysterious transcendence that reaches beyond finite human comprehension to the very essence of the divine nature and God's will for humankind.

Both Jesus and Paul shared similar views of Torah. They both treasured their heritage as Jews. In reality, they both should be described as Jewish theologians.[3] Though this may seem obvious, questions, doubts, and prejudices persist in Christian thinking regarding Jesus' and Paul's relationship to the Judaism of their day. Both of them possessed an understanding of Torah that reflected the Jewish values of the first century.[4] Was Jesus faithful to Judaism in his interpretation of Torah? Did Paul change the meaning of Torah for a new age? Our answers to these questions reveal our view of the Bible. They also say something about our relationship with the Jewish community and our attitude toward their faith. Paul interpreted the Bible like a first-century Pharisee. Before the incident on the road to Damascus, the five books of Moses were at the core of his theology. After that experience, Torah and Jesus constituted the core. Can we truly esteem Paul and think lowly of the foundation—the teachings of Torah—to which his theology was riveted? Moreover, Jesus himself upheld a high view of Torah, especially in the Sermon on the Mount. Paul reflected Jesus' view when he wrote that through faith "we uphold the law" (Rom 3:31; cf. Matt 5:17).

Jesus and Paul were both devoted to Judaism. They had similar views of Torah, but Paul worked among the Gentiles in the Diaspora, while Jesus lived among his own people in Israel. Marcion, on the other hand, hated the Hebrew Scriptures, which were sacred to the Jewish people. He opposed the Judaism of Jesus and Paul. For Marcion, Moses brought condemnation, but Paul enabled men and women to discover God's grace; Jesus' message had been perverted by his Jewish disciples, but Paul had made known the truth by revelation knowledge. Though Marcion was condemned as a heretic and excommunicated from the church about 144 CE, his special approach to Paul and the Bible entice many Christian thinkers who feel uncomfortable with the Jewish roots of Jesus' early followers. In their view, Paul removed the yoke of Judaism by preaching against the law.

THE JUDAISM OF JESUS AND PAUL

Paul's words are quoted and misquoted. In particular, Marcion-like distortions of the apostle's message are still circulating. Nevertheless, Paul's message must be interpreted in the light of the thought world that nourished it. This is especially true for the letter to the Romans. As noted in the previous chapter, Paul emphasizes his esteem for Torah when he writes to the believers in Rome, "Do we then overthrow the law [Torah] by this faith? By no means! On the contrary, we uphold the law [Torah]" (Rom 3:31). The New English Bible renders the verse, "Does this mean that we are using faith to undermine the law? By no means: we are placing law [Torah] itself on a firmer footing." The words "place on a firmer footing" is a far better translation of the meaning of the words in Greek. The Greek term *histēmi,* "stand" or "place on a firmer footing," is the equivalent of the Hebrew word *kiyem,* "cause to stand" or "make to stand through proper interpretation." Paul desired to place Torah on a firmer footing through faith.

Jesus himself used similar language in his exposition of the law when he said, "Think not that I am come to abolish the law and the prophets; I have not come to abolish but to fulfill them" (Matt 5:17). Compare the word "abolish" with Paul's use of the word "overthrow" (or "undermine"). Moreover, note the even closer relationship between "fulfill" and Paul's "uphold" (or "place on a firmer footing").[5] One upholds the law by giving it the proper interpretation, which brings about the actualization of Torah in daily living. Jesus stressed that "till heaven and earth shall pass away, not an iota, not a dot, will pass from the law . . ." (Matt 5:18).

Though heaven and earth still stand, sometimes we as Christians have inclined toward Marcion's interpretation of the gospel. Yet Paul upheld the law (Torah) by his faith in Jesus. The apostle sought to fulfill the true meaning of the Bible's teachings through the power of the Spirit. He did not cancel the Old Testament by preaching about the grace of God; rather, he correctly interpreted it. Paul placed Torah on a firmer footing by striving for a greater awareness of God. The Hebrew writings of Torah are imbued with the message of divine grace. The Lord is full of grace, compassion, and loving kindness.[6] Furthermore, the Jewish sages, so near to Jesus and Paul, heightened the message of divine grace through their unique method of reading the Bible. Jesus and Paul, like many of their contemporaries, emphasized God's goodness and grace. When it comes to Torah, both Jesus and Paul sought to fulfill the law and to obey God's will as it is revealed in the sacred text of the Hebrew Bible.

The disciples of Marcion were so troubled by this saying of Jesus that they changed the words to read, "Think not that I have come to fulfill the law but to destroy it . . ."[7] They simply inverted the words *fulfill* and *destroy* to suit their theology. Indeed, recourse to such a radical change to the text would not be endorsed by modern Christians. The words of Jesus however, frequently are interpreted to mean that the law is fulfilled, in the sense that Torah is no longer valid because of Jesus' vicarious sufferings. The methods differ but the results are similar.

In the early church the tension between law and grace was at the forefront of discussion, particularly as it pertained to non-Jewish believers who were not circumcised and who were largely ignorant of the Jewish way of life. The Jerusalem council considered the question and determined that although no person can achieve salvation through circumcision, in other words, by obeying the law, the ethics of the Jewish way of life could not be excluded.[8] The non-Jews were not required to be circumcised and to obey all the commandments of Torah. But they were expected to abandon all idolatrous practices and live ethical and moral lives.

Salvation is a gift of God that cannot be earned. No person is able to make God love him or her more than God already does. The most wretched of human beings cannot repulse God's love. The divine compassion is unconditional and un-merited. The grace of God, however, does not invite unethical or improper behavior. Paul does not advocate that one should continue in sin in order to enjoy the overabundance of divine grace. The love of God changes the heart. The individual who encounters God, who experiences his overwhelming grace, should live a life pleasing to God. Grace is found in the law, and law is found in grace.

THE TORAH IN ACTION

In the teachings of Jesus, the good works of his followers are compared to light: "Let your light so shine before men, that they may see your good works and give glory to your Father who is in heaven."[9] Jesus never taught that grace had replaced the need for good works. He compared the disciple who put his teaching into practice to a source of light. For Jesus, light was Torah in action.

In addition, Paul spoke of the law as being "spiritual." He desired that people would be empowered to fulfill the law, not by the flesh—an impossibility—but by the spirit through faith in Jesus (see Rom 8:2). For Paul, the evil of sin resides in the flesh of a person whose conduct may be controlled by his or her inclination to disobey God's command. This individual becomes a servant of sin. Faith in Jesus and the power of the Holy Spirit in the life of the believer liberates that person from slavery to the power of sin.

The rabbis often compared Torah to light. The living word of God transcends present physical reality, revealing divine ways. The rabbis did not teach a salvation-by-works religion. After painstaking analysis, E. P. Sanders concluded:

The view that Rabbinic religion was a religion of legalistic works-righteousness in which a man was saved by fulfilling more commandments than he committed transgressions I have argued is completely wrong: it proceeds from theological presuppositions and is supported by systematically misunderstanding and misconstruing passages in Rabbinic literature.[10]

Each individual must obey God's law, but he or she is saved by God's unmerited grace—not by works.

MOSES, THE LIGHT, AND THE DIVINE SPIRIT

Just as Jesus compared the disciples' good works to a shining light, so the ancient rabbis spoke about good deeds that help others. These actions of mercy result from obedience to the teachings of Torah. The rabbis compared Moses to a light. In the colorful words of comparison, the rabbis taught:

To what may Moses be compared at that time? To a light which is set upon a lamp stand from which many lights are ignited. Nothing is lacking from this light in the same way as nothing was lacking in the wisdom of Moses.[11]

Moses showed the way to greater fulfillment in life through obedience to God's way. Moses made disciples. The teaching of Torah must be studied and interpreted in a way that captures the force of God's will in daily living. This type of power flows from the divine Spirit, which enables the person to live for God in the same way that Moses, as a prophet, experienced the Holy Spirit's empowerment for effective service.

In the first century, the Jewish thinker Philo of Alexandria captured the meaning of the prophetic inspiration of Moses. The Holy Spirit inspired Moses with God's message. The seventy elders were also given divine wisdom as they studied Torah, learning from the prophet Moses. Like the rabbinic commentary cited above, Philo compares Torah to a fire that ignites many torches in the same way that Moses taught the elders Torah and they too received a portion of the divine Spirit.

> Such a divine spirit, too, is that of Moses, which visits the seventy elders that they may excel others and be brought to something better—those seventy who cannot be in real truth even elders, if they have not received a portion of that spirit of perfect wisdom. For it is written, "I will take of the spirit that is on thee and lay it upon the seventy elders" (Numb. xi. 17). But think not that this taking of the spirit comes to pass as when men cut away a piece and sever it. Rather it is, as when they take fire from fire, for though the fire should kindle a thousand torches, it is still as it was and is diminished not a whit. Of such a sort also is the nature of knowledge. All those who resort to it become its disciples, it makes into men of skill, yet no part of it is diminished.[12]

The Jewish people during the time of Jesus had refined their understanding of Torah. Within this broader tradition of seeking God's higher purposes, both Jesus and Paul desired to uphold the law by interpreting it properly. Their approaches did not violate the spirit of first-century Judaism. Jesus did not cancel the Ten Commandments when he preached. Rather, he taught that one must take extreme caution not to disobey even the least of the commandments because such an action could lead to violation of a weighty precept of the law.[13] Jesus taught that his followers should place the light upon a lamp stand for all to see.[14] Torah in action provides a strong beacon of light for a hurting world of searching people.

Out of a sincere attempt to make sense of the new faith, Marcion worked to cancel the law. His labors reflect an anti-Jewish prejudice that can be viewed as a form of nascent anti-Semitism. Others unwittingly following in his footsteps have forgotten that ancient Judaism and the Torah upon which it was based teach grace but do not remove the responsibility of faithful obedience to God. Jesus emphasized good works in his teaching, and Paul held Torah in high esteem. Marcion, however, distorted both of their messages, and his doctrine still penetrates Christian theology.

The pious acts of Jesus' disciples were not performed in order to earn divine acceptance or forgiveness. Salvation is not by works. When the message of Jesus is put into operation, the works of his disciples are a light. How can one have faith in the goodness of God without corresponding actions? Torah is light, and all who follow Jesus must not only hear the word but also live the life of obedience. These are the wise who build upon a firm foundation.

The ancient rabbis understood the need for following Moses, the great teacher of the divine purpose. Moses is like a light placed upon the lamp stand. From this light, many other lights have been set on fire. The faithful followers of Moses' teachings have brought light into the world by helping others in obedience to God's commandments.

SLAVES OF RIGHTEOUSNESS

Marcion distorted the teachings of Paul about Torah. He rejected Judaism and its strong faith in the goodness of God. Christianity in its self-definitions must never define itself as the antithesis of Judaism. Paul viewed righteousness as a way of life. The power of God is discovered in the divine righteousness. It is a force that leads to a closer relationship with one's Creator. Paul was not against the law. He desired the force of righteousness to transform his life. Paul believed in moral and ethical behavior that resulted from the Spirit-filled life. In Galatians 5, Paul describes the fruit of the Spirit in the life of the believer. In a pneumatic approach to life, the path of Torah will be followed by the person who is guided and directed by the Holy Spirit. Torah should be upheld by the preaching of faith, and the force of the divine presence in a person's life should lead the individual into a righteous lifestyle. Righteousness possesses an intense power that will lead a person unto holiness. Perhaps this is what Paul means when he exclaims with gratitude,

> But thanks be to God, that you who were once slaves of sin have become obedient from the heart to the standard of teaching to which you were committed, and, having been set free from sin, have become slaves of righteousness. (Rom 6:17–18)

Paul's use of the term "righteousness of God" embraces loving obedience to God's will. The light of Torah can be seen in the good works of Jesus' disciples. It can also be seen in Paul's epistles. Jesus and Paul possess high esteem for Torah as revealing divine grace. Torah is light. Torah possesses a transcendence that moves from one's human limitations into the divine realm. Torah is limitless. Its radiance is best seen in the actions of those who gain wisdom from studying its words. The followers of Jesus and Paul place the light upon a lamp stand when they put the teaching of Torah into practice—when, after hearing the words of Torah, they do them.

THE TRANSCENDENCE OF TORAH IN PAUL'S TEACHINGS: NOTES

1. See John Stendahl, "With Luther/Against Luther," *Explorations* 9, no. 3 (1995) 7. A dedicated Lutheran pastor, Stendahl reports how the 1993 Assembly of the Evangelical Lutheran Church in America voted to repudiate these anti-Semitic writings of Martin Luther, which were penned in 1534. Now, some 459 years later, the Lutheran Church has disclaimed these obscene declarations of vehement hate. In his celebrated historical account of World War II, *The Rise and Fall of the Third Reich* (New York: Simon and Schuster, 1960) 236, William Shirer quoted Luther and observed that the highly regarded Christian leader's advice "was literally followed four centuries later by Hitler, Goering and Himmler." Early in his ministry, Luther longed to convert the Jews to Christianity. When his attempts failed, he became filled with hatred. On the positive side, Luther's profound theological contributions must be acknowledged. The

Assembly of Evangelical Lutheran Churches possesses much tradition of which it may be proud. The churches must also be esteemed for repudiating their founder's hate-filled words for the Jewish people.

2. See the very important treatment of Marcion's thought in Harnack, *Marcion*. See also Quasten, *Patrology*, 2.273, who notes the contributions of Tertullian's arguments against Marcion:

> Altogether it consists of five books [Tertullian's *Against Marcion*], of which the first refutes the dualism existing according to Marcion between the God of the Old and the God of the New Testament and proves that the very concept of the Deity is incompatible with such a contrast. "The Christian verity has distinctly declared this principle, 'God is not, if He is not one,' because we more properly believe that that has no existence which is not as it ought to be. . . . That being which is the great Supreme, must needs be unique, by having no equal, and so not ceasing to be the great Supreme' (I, 3). Thus the Maker of the world is identical with the good God . . ."

3. See Young, *Jesus the Jewish Theologian*, 264–69; cf. also *Lev. Rab.* 19:2. R. Simeon taught:

> The Book of Deuteronomy ascended and prostrated itself before the Holy One, blessed be He, saying to Him: "Lord of the Universe, Solomon has uprooted me and made of me an invalid document, since a document out of which two or three points are void is entirely void, and King Solomon sought to uproot the letter *yod* out of me: It is written, 'He should not multiply (*lo yarbeh*) horses to himself' (Deut. XVII, 16) and he has multiplied horses to himself; it is written, 'Neither shall he multiply wives to himself' (ib. 17) and he has multiplied wives to himself; it is written, 'Neither shall he greatly multiply to himself silver and gold' (ib.) and he has multiplied silver and gold to himself." The Holy One, blessed be He, answered: "Go! Solomon will be eliminated and a hundred like him, but not even a single *yod* that is in thee shall ever be made void."

4. See Urbach, *The Sages*, 286–399.

5. See Bivin and Blizzard, *Understanding the Difficult Words of Jesus*, 80, 152–55.

6. See, e.g., Exod 34:6; Ps 103:2–5.

7. Blackman, *Marcion and His Influence*, 50.

8. Acts 15.

9. Matt 5:16.

10. Sanders, *Paul and Palestinian Judaism,* 233; cf. also Howard, "Christ the End of the Law." He observes (p. 333), "The fact is that most sects of Judaism believed very much in salvation by grace. This concept permeated the whole of Judaism in all of its divisions."

11. *Sifre Num* 93 (Horovitz, 94); and also *Sifre Zuta* on Num 11:17 (Horovitz, 271). See esp. Young, *Jesus and His Jewish Parables,* 100–101, 127 n. 148, which discusses this rabbinic parable and its parallels.

12. See Philo, *On the Giants* 24–25, in *Philo* (trans. Colson), 2.456–59. I am grateful to Joseph Frankovic, who called my attention to this parallel for the text in *Sifre Num* 93.

13. See esp. Matt 5:17–48. The best treatment of this gospel text is found in Flusser, *Judaism and the Origins of Christianity,* 494–508. For a descriptive bibliography, see also W. Kissinger, *The Sermon on the Mount* (Metuchen, N.J.: Scarecrow, 1975).

14. Matt 5:14–16; Luke 8:16, 11, 33; Mark 4:21.

Love as the Foundation of Christian Ministry: The Model of 1 Corinthians 13

*Paul's fundamental premise was quite different from theirs.
He believed that by Jesus' action the salvation promised to
Israel was made accessible even to non-Jews. Moreover,
contrary to Jewish proselytism, Paul held that Gentiles
need not first become Jewish in order to attain salvation:
they were free from the law and circumcision. Paulinism
proclaims that those who were "far from the salvation of
the Jews" have been "brought near" in Christ. The one God
is not the God of only one people; he embraces all men and
women and all nations. Universal love does not permit
exclusion of one's fellow from the community.*

Edward Schillebeeckx
Paul the Apostle

PAUL'S so-called love chapter in 1 Corinthians 13 has become famous for its beautiful style, all-consuming theme, and lofty imagery. Today it is sometimes a text of Scripture that is read at weddings. Indeed, frequently it has been removed from its historical setting and given new applications. The love chapter's placement within Paul's epistle to the Corinthians has puzzled some fine biblical scholars, who have even suggested that it was originally written independently of its present context.

Was 1 Corinthians 13 written by Paul? Did he rewrite someone else's praise of wisdom or love for his own purpose? Was it originally placed here? Was it written earlier and adapted by Paul to fit in between chapters 12 and 14, which treat questions relating to spiritual giftings for the congregation?[1] Only a new direction in Pauline studies that focuses upon his Jewish heritage can solve these perplexing problems. Here we will view the background of 1 Cor 13:12 for a fresh look at Paul's theology. There the apostle writes, "For now we see in a mirror [glass lens] dimly, but then face to face."[2] A careful analysis of the text in light of its Jewish roots reveals how closely the love chapter is connected to the manifestations of the Spirit so articulately defined and discussed in 1 Corinthians 12 and 14.

PROPHECY AND THE HOLY SPIRIT

The supernatural gifts and ministries of the Holy Spirit were a hallmark of early Christianity.[3] Some circles, however, during the time of Jesus taught that prophetic utterance and the supernatural work of the Spirit had passed away with the death of the prophets.[4] According to this view, after the death of the great prophets of the Old Testament, the people had to rely upon the uncertain guidance of what was called the daughter voice (*bat kol*), or echo from heaven, which could be related to a heavenly voice like that heard at Jesus' baptism or even to the whisper of a child.[5] Prophecy, however, was closely related to the movement of the Holy Spirit. Indeed, the term *prophecy* itself often denoted the gift of the Spirit that was designed to deliver God's message. Hence, guidance and encouragement for the community were given through prophetic utterance by the power of the Spirit.

Still other Jewish circles believed that prophecy continued to be in operation. The movement of early Christianity was characterized by the guidance and the manifestation of the Spirit. The book of Acts consistently describes the work of the Holy Spirit, which guides the church. On the day of Pentecost, the Spirit was given, which in part was an indication that indeed the days of the Messiah had come.

GIFTINGS OF THE SPIRIT AT CORINTH

In his Corinthian correspondence, Paul deals with a number of complex problems menacing the congregation that he founded (Acts 18). One of the chief controversies focused upon the use and the abuse of spiritual manifestations. First Corinthians 12 and 14 treat these issues in great depth. The great love chapter serves as a bridge between these two passages. Hence, the question must be asked: Is 1 Corinthians 13 primarily concerned with the works and operations of the Spirit within the local church? Scholarly answers to the question have been ambivalent.

When Paul writes, "For now we see in a mirror [glass lens] dimly, but then face to face," he is hinting at the Hebrew Scriptures. Familiarity with early Jewish thought, moreover, illuminates the meaning of the term *mirror*, which probably refers to a type of primitive glass lens used to make distant objects clearer.[6] But first it should be observed that the entire passage in 1 Corinthians 13 makes numerous references to tongues, prophecy, faith, and knowledge, among other things, but above all points to the more excellent way. Love must guide the direction of ministry in the local congregation as the excellent way. Obviously, these references to the manifestations of the Spirit echo Paul's writing in 1 Corinthians 12 and 14. But what does Paul mean by the imagery of "mirror [lens]," "dimly," and "face to face"?

MOSES AND THE PROPHETS

Here Paul is alluding to a specific passage of Torah that uses the same words as 1 Cor 13:12 as it describes Moses and the other prophets. According to Jewish tradition, Moses was the first and the greatest of the prophets. The Holy Spirit inspires and guides the prophets. Moses not only was known as a lawgiver but, much more so, as a prophet who spoke for the Lord. All the prophets were directed by the Holy Spirit, but Moses communicated with God on a more intimate level. In Num 12:6–8, the Lord speaks and contrasts the difference between Moses and the other prophets:

> Hear my words: If there is a prophet among you, I the LORD make myself known to him in a vision, I speak with him in a dream. Not so my servant Moses; he is entrusted with all my house. With him I speak mouth to mouth, clearly, and not in dark speech; and he beholds the form of the LORD.

Notably, in the Septuagint's translation of the Hebrew text, the same Greek word is used for "dark speech" in Num 12:8 as is used for "dimly" in 1 Cor 13:12. The idea conveyed is one of imperfection or simply of incompleteness. The precise meaning for the word of the Lord remains enigmatic or somewhat of a riddle. Prophecy is not always crystal clear. In contrast to others, however, Moses was a prophet who spoke with God "mouth to mouth" and even viewed the form of the Lord. The Hebrew language is fond of idioms that metaphorically refer to parts of the physical body, such as "mouth to mouth" or "face to face" (see Deut 34:10). Moses enjoyed a close and personal communication with God, which granted him a surer word of prophecy. Significantly, Paul refers to the fact that we now peer through the mirror or glass lens dimly, but then "face to face." The Hebrew idiom "face-to-face" is like "mouth-to-mouth." Thus, it seems clear that Paul is alluding to Num 12:8. He is referring to Moses and prophecy. But what is meant by the term *glass,* or *mirror?*

THE MIRROR OR LENS FOR PROPHECY

Judah bar Ilai, a famous rabbi from the beginning of the second century, quoted Num 12:8 in a similar discussion concerning Moses, the gift of prophecy, and the other prophets. Moreover, he employs the term *glass,* or *mirror.* His definition of the word can provide deeper insights into Paul's chapter about love and spiritual gifts. Below is his answer to the question "What is the difference between Moses and all the prophets?"

> Through nine mirrors [lenses] did the prophets behold [prophetic visions]. This is indicated by what is said, "And the appearance of the vision which I saw, was like the vision that I saw when I came to destroy the city; and the visions were like the vision that I saw by the River Chebar; and I fell upon my face" (Ezek 43:3);[7] but Moses beheld [prophetic visions] through one mirror [lens], as it is said "With him do I speak mouth to mouth, clearly, and not in dark speech" (Numbers 12:8). The Rabbis said: All the other prophets beheld prophetic visions through a blurred mirror [lens]. . . . But Moses beheld [prophetic visions] through a polished mirror [lens] as it is said, "He beholds the form of the LORD (Numbers 12:8)."[8]

In this passage from rabbinic literature, the mirror or lens refers to prophetic utterance and the giving of the Holy Spirit.[9] The other prophets see through a dirty mirror or a lens that is clouded. But Moses sees through a clean glass lens and receives clearly the prophetic message from the Holy Spirit. The glass brings what is far away and indistinct into focus. Hence, the mirror or lens refers to an instrument or a means through which the divine will or message becomes manifest. The imagery is intended to convey the idea of focusing on God himself. On the other hand, the so-called gifts of the Spirit, as described in 1 Corinthians 12 and 14, are instruments for the local church, in operation in the Christian community at Corinth. But they are like unpolished mirrors or primitive glass lenses through which the people behold the form of the Lord.

The problem was the human element in the working of the Holy Spirit. Manipulative self-interests were now motivating the people rather than pure selfless love. Though the manifestations of the Spirit were given for the common good (1 Cor 12:7), Christians at Corinth were exploiting them. Jealousy, as well as other human weaknesses, had caused the genuine love and concern for the needs of the community to fade.

Paul, as the founder of the church, writes to his brothers and sisters out of a deep pastoral concern. These spiritualities (mirrors or glass lenses) are manifested to upbuild the whole congregation and not to exalt one member of the body over the rest. The love chapter is the pivotal point of Paul's message in 1 Corinthians 12–14. These three chapters were meant to be studied together, not as independent units. Love, as a fruit of the Spirit, must guide and govern the other manifestations. What contributes most to all the members of the church must be considered the most important. Paul stresses faith, hope, and love (1 Cor 13:13). All the imperfect divine manifestations of the Spirit will become superfluous when the Lord returns and completes his messianic task. Paul warns the congregation, "as for prophecies, they will pass away . . . but when the perfect comes, the imperfect will pass away" (1 Cor 13:8–10). All creation longs for that day (Rom 8:18–25). Everything moves toward the goal set by God. Love will abide even when the other instruments fade away because of the awesome glory of his coming. The "perfect" manifestations—namely, the apocalyptic coming of the messiah and the complete spiritual restoration that will accompany his appearance—will abolish the need for other manifestations of the Spirit. Why? Because at that time God's people will see face to face. Compared with the completeness of his coming, the present spiritualities resemble dirty mirrors, imperfect lenses, dark speeches, and blurred vision. In the same way that the other prophets fade in their brilliance when compared to Moses, the present spiritual manifestations fail in comparison with the future glory that will be seen at the Parousia.

So with wisdom Paul counsels his church, "Make love your aim, and earnestly desire the spiritual gifts" (1 Cor 14:1). He encourages people to desire the gifts, but only as a means to greater service. Seeking the giftings of the Spirit out of love, out of a desire to minister to those in need more efficiently, is the apostle's noble concern.[10] Love for others must be seen as the more excellent way. Love is the bridge between the empowerment of the Spirit and the help one gives to people with serious human needs. Love must characterize the ministry of the individual Christian as well as the whole Christian community. Love must be the basis of ministry in the local congregation. The message of Paul in 1 Corinthians 13 is an essential nexus between chapters 12 and 14. Without love the most powerful spiritual manifestations are entirely meaningless. Certainly the words of Paul are closely related to the words of Jesus, recorded in John's Gospel, "By this all men will know that you are my disciples, if you have love for one another" (John 13:35).

LOVE AS THE FOUNDATION OF CHRISTIAN MINISTRY: NOTES

1. See Fee, *The First Epistle to the Corinthians*, 625–52. See J. T. Sanders, "First Corinthians 13, Its Interpretation Since the First World War," *Interpretation* 20 (1966) 159–87. Sanders believes the chapter has been placed in its present context by a redactor. Conzelmann and Wischmeyer view it as a revision of an earlier literary work because of similar parallels; see H. Conzelmann, *1 Corinthians* (Hermeneia; Philadelphia: Fortress, 1975) 217–20; and O. Wischmeyer, *Der höchster Weg* (Gütersloh, Gütersloher Verlagshaus Mohn, 1981). Consider E. L. Titus, "Did Paul Write I Corinthians 13?" *Journal of Bible and Religion* 27 (1959) 299–302.

2. Here we shall argue that "lens" is likely a better translation than "mirror" in 1 Cor 13:12. The rabbinic parallels support this interpretation. There is even a reference in Pliny that describes Nero watching the gladiatorial battles through some type of glass. Though the evidence is inconclusive, it may well be that already in the time of Paul many people would have used some type of magnifying glasses or lenses to improve vision or even to start a fire. In a fine study given to me by Joseph Frankovic, "*Aspak-*

larya," in *Sefer Hayovel Leprofesor Shmuel Kraus* (Hebrew; Jerusalem: Rubin Mass, 1936) 10–14, Immanuel Leif discusses the evidence in Jewish and Roman literatures.

3. See E. E. Ellis, *Pauline Theology* (Grand Rapids: Eerdmans, 1989). Ellis observes, "For the Apostle Paul the gifts of the Holy Spirit are the essence of Christian ministry, and apart from these gifts ministry in its essential character does not take place" (p. 52).

4. See E. Urbach, "The *Shekhina*—the Presence of God in the World," in *The Sages,* vol. 1, 37–65; and "Matay Paskah Hanevuah?" *Tarbitz* 17 (1945–46) 1–11 (Hebrew).

5. See S. Lieberman, *Hellenism in Jewish Palestine* (New York, 1962) 194–99.

6. Cf. Leif, *"Aspaklarya,"* 13.

7. The number nine is based upon how many times the concept of prophetic vision appears in Ezek 43:3. Here the word *vision* is derived from the Hebrew root *ra'ah* "to see." A prophet is sometimes called a seer.

8. *Lev. Rab.* 1:14 (Margulies, 1.30); English translation, *Midrash Rabbah* (Soncino), 4.17. The classic treatment of the Holy Spirit in rabbinic literature presently is Peter Schäfer, *Die Vorstellung vom Heiligen Geist in der rabbinischen Literatur* (Munich: Kösel, 1972). See also Michael E. Lodahl, *The Shekhinah/Spirit: Divine Presence in Jewish and Christian Religion* (New York: Paulist, 1992).

9. See Brad H. Young, "The Ascension Motif of 2 Corinthians 12 in Jewish, Christian and Gnostic Texts," *Grace Theological Journal* 9 (1, 1988) 73–103. Of monumental importance for the larger context in the Gospels is Notley, "The Concept of the Holy Spirit."

10. See also Ridderbos, *Paul: An Outline of His Theology,* 201–2.

9 The Essence of Paul's Jewish Faith

The burning question among Jewish Christians was, "Has God rejected his people?" (Rom 11:1). Paul devoted three whole chapters to this problem and concluded that finally the natural branches (Jews) which had been broken off the olive tree (the people of God) would be grafted back onto the tree: "so all Israel will be saved" (Rom 11:26). It is difficult to interpret these three chapters symbolically of the church—the spiritual Israel. They teach that literal Israel is yet to be included in spiritual Israel.

George Eldon Ladd
A Commentary on the Revelation of John

L IKE other Pharisees, Paul might have summarized the essence of his faith in the verse "Hear, O Israel, the LORD our God, the LORD is one" (Deut 6:4). Christians routinely view Judaism from the time of Jesus as a religion of merit. We wrongly assume that the essence of Judaism in Paul's day taught that a person must earn his or her salvation by complete obedience to the law. To use Paul's analogy from Romans 9–11, we forget the roots of our faith. We vainly imagine that we support the root. As the wild olive shoot that was grafted into the tree, we cut off the limb upon which we sit. Down we fall as we arrogantly characterize ancient Jewish faith and practice as a salvation-by-works religion. As Christians, we must not sever ourselves from the tree into which we have been grafted contrary to nature. Jewish belief begins with the proper understanding of God's nature. We must learn to appreciate the root that supports us.

Tragedy emerges when we study the historical records documenting the relationship between the church and synagogue. Many chapters are blotted by red-colored stains—the blood of pious Jews. How can we Christians understand our own faith in God when we have cut ourselves off from our Jewish heritage? The essence of Jewish faith is contained in its understanding of the divine nature. God is good. He is holy. He is one. Christian theological discussion, in its polemical reflection on the faith of the people of Israel, has often distorted the clear concept of God that is expressed in the core of Jewish belief.[1] The misconception that Judaism preaches a message of salvation by works has undermined the rich heritage of the Hebrew Scriptures, which both Christians and Jews hold sacred.[2] The Christian faith rests upon its concept of the nature of God. Faith in Jesus should not contradict the faith *of* Jesus. Indeed, the all-pervasive root of Jewish belief, "Hear, O Israel, the LORD our God, the LORD is one," is taught throughout the New Testament itself.

Here we will explore two questions: First, what is the Jewish concept of God? Second, what does the New Testament teach about the nature of the one God from the Hebrew Scriptures? Today we should not be surprised to discover that the ancient affirmation known as the *Shema Yisrael* ("Hear, O Israel") was an all-pervading doctrine for the leaders of the early church.

When reciting in prayer these words, how did the Jewish people in Jesus' day understand the nature of God? The Jewish concept of God is closely tied to the concept of the kingdom of heaven (Hebrew, *malchut shamayim*). The rabbis believed that when a person prayed the *Shema Yisrael*, he or she was affirming genuine faith in the only God. Moreover, by praying the Shema, the individual was rejecting the idolatrous beliefs of the pagan world, which recognized many gods. Greco-Roman society was a culture thriving on a plurality of gods and assorted religious philosophies. Polytheism was accepted belief and practice during the New Testament period and the talmudic age. In modern Western society, the notion of polytheism is rejected theologically but still can be practiced religiously. At least the danger of false worship, which elevates a person or thing above God, is always real. In the ancient prayers of the Jewish people, the Shema was recited twice a day.[3] The Hebrew words of the prayer would have been upon the lips of every pious worshiper during the days of the Second Temple. Jesus himself would have prayed the Shema. Paul prayed the Hebrew prayers of the ancient synagogue and participated in the glorious worship of the temple in Jerusalem. Paul entered fully into the celebration of the Jewish feasts and festivals. The same was true for Peter, James, John, and the rest of the early followers of Jesus.

The oral Jewish tradition preserved in the talmudic literature discusses the significance of the prayer. The Shema is made up of three sections of Scripture—Deut 6:4–9, 11:12–22, and Num 15:37–42. Unfortunately, we as Christians seldom associate these key passages with the beliefs of the early church. No doubt Jesus and all his disciples were able to recite these passages by heart in Hebrew at a very tender age. In his commentary on the Jewish prayers, Joseph Hertz explains, "These are foundation pillars of the Jewish Faith."[4] The Shema, he stresses, "is a proclamation of the existence and Unity of God; of Israel's complete loyalty to God and His commandments; the belief in Divine Justice; the remembrance of the liberation from Egypt, and its corollary, the Election of Israel."[5] The first section of the Shema, from Deut 6:4–9, focuses upon the divine nature and emphasizes the need for every individual to love and reverence the Lord, who is one. The love of God must be taught in the family and passed on to every child. The second section, from Deut 11:13–22, begins with the words "And if you will obey my commandments which I command you this day, to love the LORD your God, and to serve him with all your heart and with all your soul." This section emphasizes the urgency of obedience to the Lord. To love God is to obey him. The third section, from Num 15:37–41, concludes with the remembrance of God's mighty act of redemption when he liberated the people of Israel from slavery: "I am the LORD your God, who brought you out of the land of Egypt to be your God; I am the LORD your God." Faith is remembering. When one recalls the mighty acts of God in the past, one builds faith for present needs. The people experienced God's love as he worked miracles to save them—past, present, and future.

An important Jewish teacher who lived not long after Jesus, Joshua ben Korcha, asked, "Why does the [first] section, 'Hear, O Israel, the LORD our God, the LORD is one' (Deut. 6:4), precede the [second] section, 'And if you will obey my commandments which I command you this day, to love the LORD your God . . .' (Deut. 11:13)?" The question is very much to the point. Why are these blocks of Scripture combined to formulate a liturgical prayer that must be recited twice daily? The answer Joshua ben Korcha gave is simple but profound: "The kingdom of heaven." He declared that Deut 6:4–9 precedes the recitation of Deut 11:13–22 "so that individuals may first take upon themselves the kingdom of heaven and afterward take upon themselves the yoke of the commandments."[6] The rule of God is related to the human response to the divine initiative. God has reached out to all people by his mighty acts of salvation and has provided a higher way of life for the subjects of his kingdom. The reign of God is realized among people as they experience his mighty power and obey his will. Obedience to God's way of life is the natural response to the divine nature. Ephraim Urbach makes it clear: "The acceptance of the yoke of the kingdom of heaven means to acknowledge that God is One and Unique, and to bear witness that there is no other god."[7]

THE POWER OF GOD'S REIGN

In the parables, the rabbis preached about the pivotal significance of God's reign. The kingdom signifies God's redemptive power. His rule encompasses the authority of Torah. At Sinai, the people of Israel received the Ten Commandments with joy because already they had experienced divine deliverance and protection.

> They told a parable: To what may the matter be compared? To one who came to a province. He said to the people, "May I reign over you?" They said to him, "You have done nothing good for us that we should accept your reign!" What did he do? He built them a wall. He brought them water. He fought battles for them. Then he said to them, "May I reign over you?" They responded, "Yes! Yes!" Thus it was with the Omnipresent. He redeemed Israel from Egypt. He parted the sea for them. He brought them manna. He provided them with a well. He sent them quail. He fought the battle of Amalek for them. He said to them, "May I reign over you?" They replied, "Yes! Yes!" Rabbi said, "This shows the grace of Israel. When they stood before Mount Sinai to receive the Torah, they all determined in their hearts to accept the Kingdom of heaven with joy."[8]

The New Testament teachings about the nature of God are firmly rooted in the Hebrew Scriptures and paralleled in rabbinic thought. The Jewish background of early Christianity provides an enriched perception of the significance of God's oneness in Christian faith and practice. In his epistle, James, who is believed to be the half brother of Jesus, writes, "You believe that God is one . . ." (Jas 2:19).[9] This declaration had profound meaning for all the people who prayed the Shema twice each day as a devout expression of their strong faith in God. Stressing that faith without works is dead, James challenges his readers from the twelve tribes of the Diaspora (Jas 1:1). One does not earn one's salvation by good deeds, but true faith is accompanied by corresponding actions. Faith is active. Belief in the one God will result in a life of committed service and unyielding devotion to him. James refers to Abraham, who because of his faith obeyed God and offered Isaac: "You see that faith was active along with his works, and faith was completed by works, and the scripture was fulfilled which says, 'Abraham believed God, and it was reckoned to him as righteousness' " (Jas 2:22).

The theology of Joshua ben Korcha is very similar. At least one point of convergence is discovered between Joshua ben Korcha and James. Joshua ben Korcha teaches that when an individual prays, "Hear O Israel, the LORD our God, the LORD is one," he or she accepts the kingdom of heaven and takes the first step toward a life of obedience to God. James teaches that belief in the one God must be accompanied by works because true faith will always result in corresponding action. According to James, the prominent leader in the early church, the deeper meaning of the Shema involves faithful and obedient service to God's will.

In the Gospels, Jesus was tempted by Satan (Luke 4:1–13 and parallels). The true significance of the temptation of Jesus will never be appreciated when the episode in the Gospels is divorced from its background in the Hebrew Scriptures of Deuteronomy 6, 7, and 8. The Shema from Deut 6:4 is a key passage for this event in the life of Jesus. Most students of the New Testament remember the question of the lawyer who asked Jesus about the greatest commandment—the lawyer's question was answered from Deut 6:4—but few recognize the significance of the Shema for the temptation of Jesus.[10] In the temptation story, Satan promises to surrender the rulers and kingdoms of the present world over to the authority of Jesus on one condition: "If you, then, will worship me, it shall all be yours" (Luke 4:7).

The answer Jesus gives to Satan's temptation reflects the pillar of Jewish belief, "Hear O Israel, the LORD our God, the

LORD is one." Jesus replies with, "It is written," and quotes
Deut 6:13, "You shall worship the LORD God, and him only
shall you serve." As David Flusser noted in a recent study of
this Gospel passage, the quotation from Deut 6:13 with
which Jesus answers Satan's temptation has cost many Jewish lives during the course of the history of Israel.[11] The
belief that the Lord is God and him only shall a person
serve has been defended with human life. The addition of
the word *only* to Deut 6:13 in the quotation of the Torah
passage in Luke 4:8, the temptation of Jesus, is now well
documented in Hebrew texts of Deut 6:13. The presence of
the word gives greater emphasis to the meaning of the verse as
it is quoted by Jesus.[12] The words "him *only*" remind the
listener of the Shema and the commandment "Thou shalt have
no other gods . . ." Jesus did not fall to Satan's temptation but
remained faithful to the higher purpose of the divine plan.
The message of the Shema is vital for a proper appreciation of
the Gospel story of the temptation in the life and teachings of
Jesus.[13]

The Apostle Paul also affirms the Jewish understanding of
the divine nature. Writing to the Corinthian congregation,
Paul approaches a divisive pastoral problem from the foundation of his strong faith in the Jewish understanding of God's
character. To be sure, he speaks of Jesus' own special position
in Christian faith as well (1 Cor 8:6b).[14] When the question of
food offered to an idol was raised, Paul stressed, "We know
that 'an idol has no real existence,' and that 'there is no God
but one' " (1 Cor 8:4). His entire treatment of the serious issue
confronting the believers in Corinth reaches its climax when
Paul affirms, "Yet for us there is one God, the Father, from
whom are all things and for whom we exist . . ." (1 Cor 8:6a).
The Jewish readers most naturally would hear a strong affirmation of the words "Hear O Israel, the LORD our God, the
LORD is one." Paul approaches the pastoral problems at Corinth
from a Jewish theological position.

GOD IN JEWISH THOUGHT

The Jewish concept of God and the New Testament witness to the divine nature converge at this central point of sacred doctrine, epitomized in Deut 6:4. The pervasive Hebrew heritage of the early Christians emerges in this understanding of God. Joshua ben Korcha taught that everyone who recites the Shema as the ancient affirmation of God's character has accepted the kingdom of heaven. In a Jewish text from 150 BCE, the author of the book of *Jubilees* alludes to this approach when he relates the story of Abraham's conversion to the monotheistic faith. When Abraham realized that the Lord is God, he declared, "thy kingdom I have chosen" (*Jub.* 12:19).[15] The passage in *Jubilees* clearly demonstrates that the heart of Joshua ben Korcha's teaching was well known long before the time of Jesus. Abraham recognized that the Lord is God and accepted his kingdom.

The only time a man is exempt from praying the Shema is on his wedding night. The rabbis reasoned that one would not be able to concentrate on praying the prayer with true *kavanah*, that is, proper intention of the heart. The Jewish oral law of the Mishnah taught, "A bridegroom is exempt from reciting the Shema on the first night" (*m. Ber.* 2:5). Rabban Gamaliel, however, recited the Shema even on his wedding night. When his disciples wanted to know why, their master replied, "I will not hearken to you to cast off from myself the yoke of the kingdom of heaven even for a moment."[16] Rabban Gamaliel realized that reciting the Shema was a mighty act of determination. He was receiving the kingdom of heaven and welcoming the divine presence into every aspect of his life. The great teacher of Israel would not cast off God's presence even for a brief moment.

The rich Jewish concept of the divine nature had an impact on the message and the meaning of Jesus' proclamation of the kingdom of heaven. Here we have explored the meaning of the Jewish concept of God in early Christian doctrine. The New Testament contains references to the Shema, Judaism's central doctrine, as it bears witness to the teachings of Jesus, James, and Paul. For a Jewish theologian such as Paul, a Pharisee among the Christians, Jews, and pagans, the meaning of the Shema became a foundation pillar in his teachings. Perhaps the Jewish concept of God's nature is best captured in Jesus' teaching concerning the kingdom of heaven. The kingdom refers to sovereignty. The term *heaven* means God himself. Jesus taught, "Seek ye first the kingdom of heaven and his righteousness . . ." (Matt 6:33 and parallels). One senses the keen awareness of the divine nature in this saying from the teachings of Jesus. God's sovereignty is a driving force for change, renewal, and wholeness in a world that is pulled toward the worship of many gods. God's reign in his supreme power must be understood upon the foundation of the divine character.

The firm Jewish foundations of Christian faith, with their deep roots in the Hebrew Scriptures, are seldom fully acknowledged or appreciated by the church. The Apostle Paul reminds the Romans, "They are [present tense] Israelites, and to them belong the sonship, the glory, the covenants, the giving of the law, the worship, and the promises; to them belong the patriarchs, and of their race, according to the flesh, is the Christ. God who is over all be blessed for ever. Amen" (Rom 9:4–5). While Paul warns against arrogance, he teaches the Romans to stand in awe and reverence before God: "If you do boast, remember it is not you that support the root, but the root that supports you" (Rom 11:18).[17] The concept of God in Jewish belief remains a strong pillar of faith for all Christians who desire to follow Jesus. His imperative to seek first the kingdom and God's righteousness is a powerful witness to the Jewish inception of Christianity. The sages of Israel were also fond of speaking about the kingdom of heaven. The kingdom of heaven in rabbinic teachings, on the one hand, and Jesus' message of

God's reign, on the other, give the church and the synagogue a common bond in the people's worship of the God who is revealed in the Bible they share.[18]

THE DOCTRINE OF THE RESURRECTION

In Greco-Roman thought generally, the body was thought to be the prison of the soul. Evil matter is temporal and the spirit is eternal.[19] In Gnostic religious systems, moreover, the believer required special revelation knowledge to ascend through the dangerous celestial spheres to escape from the material universe. The god of spirits—sought by Gnostics—was not interested in the revival of dead bodies. According to their religious system, the material universe was composed of evil matter, which is contrasted to the spiritual realm. Greeks longed to be free from the confines of the body. While they did believe in the survival of the human soul after death, the notion that the body would be reunited with the soul in a physical resuscitation was foreign to their conceptual world.

The Jewish people, however, believed that God created the world. Our physical world is God's creation, and it is good. The Pharisees, in contrast to the Greco-Roman religious beliefs, vigorously affirmed the doctrine of the resurrection of the dead.[20] The Pharisees stressed a literal resurrection of the physical body, which would be reunited with the spirit of an individual. Their worldview embraced a future restoration of God's original design for his world. The Pharisees envisioned a time of redemption in which God would realign the physical creation with the ethereal realm.

In teaching the resurrection, the sages of the Mishnah, who are the spiritual successors to the Pharisees, went so far as to declare, "The one who says the resurrection of the dead is not taught in the Torah, has no place in the world to come" (*m. Sanh.* 10:1). The saying is probably directed against the Sadducees. The Pharisees ardently taught the resurrection and discovered proofs from the Bible to support their position. They believed that anyone not convinced by these proof texts from the Torah would inherit not eternal life but damnation.

As we have seen, the notion of a resurrection of dead bodies was largely incompatible with the Hellenistic world view. But from within Judaism itself, the doctrine of the resurrection was opposed vigorously by the Sadducees. The Apostle Paul, however, fervently defended the doctrine in his epistle to the Corinthians. His defense is one of the most powerful and poignant arguments for the belief in the resurrection recorded anywhere in human history.[21] His argument begins with the resurrection appearances of Jesus and moves to the traditional foundation for the teaching of a bodily resurrection in the Bible and Pharisaic interpretation. For Paul, the resurrection was not merely a theological consideration; it had a practical application for him in his own personal spirituality.

The Pharisees' concept of the resurrection flowed from their interpretation of verses such as Dan 12:2, "And many of those who sleep in the dust of the earth shall awake, some to everlasting life, and some to shame and everlasting contempt." The passage reveals an eschatological reward for the righteous and severe punishment for the wicked. As in Paul's writings, the idea of a divine retribution was prevalent in Pharisaic teachings. The apostle's notion of reward and punishment in the eschatological future was rooted in his Pharisaic heritage.

In the Talmud, the heretics, who in this context were likely the Sadducees, argued with Rabbi Gamaliel about the concept of the resurrection. They maintained that the doctrine is not taught in the Bible. Rabbi Gamaliel demonstrates a Pharisaic style of hermeneutics when he locates the doctrine in all three major divisions of the Hebrew Bible—Torah, the Prophets, and the Writings:

The Sadducees [*minim*; literally, heretics] asked Rabban Gamaliel, "How do you prove that the Holy One, blessed be He, will resurrect the dead?" He answered, "From the Torah, from the Prophets, and from the Writings. From the Torah: it is written, 'And the LORD said to Moses, "Behold you are about to sleep with your fathers; but then [you] will rise [again]"' (Deut. 31:16, according to the Pharisaic interpretation!)." "But perhaps," they argued, "the text reads, 'and they shall rise up.'" [But Rabban Gamaliel countered], "Also from the Prophets: as it is written, 'Thy dead shall live, their bodies shall rise. O dwellers of the dust, awake and sing for joy! For thy dew is a dew of light, and on the land of the shades thou wilt let it fall'" (Isa. 26:19). [The Sadducees retorted,] "Perhaps this is referring to the dead who were resurrected in Ezekiel?" [Rabban Gamaliel, however, argued, "The resurrection is] also taught in the Writings, as it is written: 'and your palate like the best wine that goes down smoothly, making the lips of the sleepers to speak [or, in Pharisaic interpretation, "the sleepers" may be understood as "the deceased"]' (Songs of Solomon 7:9)."[22]

The Pharisees, therefore, sought to prove that their teachings concerning the resurrection were derived directly from the Bible. One must also remember that Jesus himself was confronted by hostile Sadducees who asked him an outlandish question about the doctrine of the resurrection.[23] They asked him a hypothetical question concerning a woman who had married a man with seven brothers. When the man died, according to levirate marriage, his wife would be given to his brother as a wife. When the second brother died, the poor woman would be married to the third in line. In this way she was passed from one brother to another until she had married each of the seven brothers. In such a case, to whom would the woman be wed at the resurrection of the dead? The episode reveals a mocking attitude. The Sadducees ask such a question because they do not believe in the doctrine of the resurrection. Very much like the Pharisees, Jesus defends the belief in the reviving of the dead by refuting their mockery. Indeed, according to the Synoptic Gospels, Jesus' faith in the resurrection of the dead was based on Torah by a Pharisaic-type interpretation. If God is referred to as the God of each of the patriarchs, he is the God of the living and not the dead. Hence, the resurrection must be a doctrine anchored in Torah.

THE SOUL AND THE BODY

In Pharisaic Judaism, the final judgment was understood as the scene of retribution for each individual. At that time both the soul and the body would be revived and judged together. The rabbis held to this belief, which is most probably derived from the Pharisees. They believed that there is an essential unity between the material body and the ethereal qualities of the human soul. In the talmudic literature, Antoninus asked Rabbi about the divine retribution, questioning how it is possible for both the soul and the body to be held responsible in the afterlife for actions done before death. Perhaps the soul would accuse the body, or the body the soul. After all, the Greeks tended to blame wrongdoing on the body only. In reply to this question of philosophical speculation, Rabbi told a parable:

> I will tell you a parable. To what may the matter be compared? To a human king who owned a beautiful orchard which contained splendid figs. Now, he appointed two watchmen therein, one lame and the other blind. [One day] the lame man said to the blind, "I see the beautiful figs in the orchard. Come and take me upon your shoulder, that we may take and eat them." So the lame bestrode the blind, took and ate them. Some time after, the owner of the orchard came and inquired of them, "Where are those beautiful figs?" The lame man replied, "Have I then feet to walk with?" The blind man replied, "Have I then eyes to see with?" What did he do? He placed the lame upon the blind and judged them together. Thus also the Holy One, blessed be He, will bring the soul, and place it in the body and judge them together . . .[24]

This famous parable is used to illustrate the divine retribution in the future. The owner of the fig orchard appointed two watchmen, one blind and the other lame, to guard his trees. His figs were being stolen. The lame could not walk to steal fruit and the blind could not see, but together they could accomplish the task of watchmen. Nonetheless, the king's fruit continued to be stolen. The wise king figured out what was happening. He placed the lame on the shoulders of the blind showing how they conspired together to steal his fruit. The eyes of the lame served the blind, and the legs of the blind assisted the lame as they both ate as much fruit as they desired. Having exposed their wrongdoing, the king judged them both as one culprit. At the resurrection, in a similar way, God will pronounce judgment on soul and body together. The rabbis saw the basic unity between the physical and the metaphysical. Interestingly, the Apostle Paul stresses the power of the Lord in the physical body. He seems to recognize a spiritual force in the physical domain. Paul teaches that the body is for the Lord because it is the temple of the Holy Spirit (1 Cor 6:19). He does not separate the body from his personal spirituality.

In affirming the Pharisaic doctrine of the resurrection, the Apostle Paul teaches that in the eschatological future, the physical and metaphysical nature of every human being will be transformed into a glorified state. One's material existence will be re-created together with one's spiritual nature—a supernatural restructuring that results in a celestial body. This eschatological reforming of the individual results in a new corporeal reality that is eternal and spiritually alive. What is perishable—a human body—will be revived in a glorified existence with an imperishable body. Paul declares, "So is it with the resurrection of the dead. What is sown is perishable, what is raised is imperishable" (1 Cor 15:42).

Paul uses the metaphor of a grain of wheat that is sown as a seed and harvested as food. In the rabbinic literature, Rabbi

Meir employs the same imagery of a wheat grain. Such similarities in metaphorical language could have arisen independently of each other, but it is also possible that the Apostle Paul and Rabbi Meir tapped an older, common tradition employed by the Pharisees to prove their case with those who ridiculed their beliefs. In talmudic literature, Queen Cleopatra asks Rabbi Meir about the appearance of the righteous when they would be raised from the dead in their revived celestial bodies.[25] Being a believer in the resurrection, she wanted to know whether they would be resurrected in the nude or with suitable clothes. Apparently the queen was a little apprehensive whether she would have to appear in the buff. Such a question seems appropriate enough for Queen Cleopatra. Rabbi Meir tells her that it is like a grain of wheat. It is sown as a seed and raised in full blossom—like the righteous in their glorious robes on the day of resurrection. He reasoned from a minor premise, the grain of wheat, to a major premise, the glorified bodies of the righteous on resurrection day.

The Apostle Paul tells the Corinthians, "And what you sow is not the body which is to be, but a bare kernel, perhaps of wheat or of some other grain. But God gives it a body as he has chosen, and each kind of seed its own body" (1 Cor 15:37–38). Rabbi Meir tells Queen Cleopatra, "If a kernel of wheat is buried naked and will sprout forth in many robes, how much more so the righteous!" (b. Sanh. 90b).

The doctrine of the resurrection was a foundation pillar of Pharisaic belief. Paul's faith in the future resurrection became a powerful motivation in his ministry. The hope of the resurrection focuses on the day in the eschatological future when, conquering the spiritual forces of evil, Jesus the Messiah will deliver the kingdom unto the Father. The resurrection of Jesus releases the force of God's sovereignty in the present. The true intensity of resurrection power, however, will only be realized in the future, when Satan's dominion is eliminated.

THE KINGDOM AND THE SPIRIT

Surely the Pharisaic doctrine of the resurrection played a leading role in the spiritual formation of the pre-Christian Paul. Furthermore, Paul's belief in the resurrection of Jesus authenticated his Pharisaic theology. The apostle's pneumatology also greatly influenced his theological development. Experientially, in his personal spiritual pilgrimage, Paul testified that he felt the same Spirit who raised the Messiah from the dead giving strength and vitality to his mortal body. Hence, from Paul's perspective, the resurrection was more than belief or dogma; its force was operative in the apostle's life and ministry in a practical way. At least in his personal life, he bore witness to these perceptions, which he believed should be normative in the experience of all Christian believers. Encouraging the believers in Rome, Paul tells them that the power of the resurrection of Jesus, the mightiest act of God—according to his mode of thinking—is even now operating in the present life: "If the Spirit of him who raised Jesus from the dead dwells in you, he who raised Christ Jesus from the dead will give life to your mortal bodies also through his Spirit which dwells in you" (Rom 8:11).

RIGHTEOUS LIVING IN THE KINGDOM

In his teachings on the kingdom of heaven, the Apostle Paul stresses a life of righteousness pleasing to God. For him, the kingdom represented a dynamic power that brought healing and wholeness. As a Pharisee, Paul would have been acquainted with the teachings of Jewish leaders connecting God's reign with praying the Shema. Acknowledging God's sovereignty breaks the power of evil in a person's life and leads the individual on to the path of righteousness. Paul recognized that many in his congregations had come from pagan backgrounds. They had been involved in sinful activities that were contrary to Jewish ethics. To encourage the Corinthians, he writes:

> Do you not know that the unrighteous will not inherit the kingdom of God? Do not be deceived; neither the immoral, nor idolaters, nor adulterers, nor sexual perverts, nor thieves, nor the greedy, nor drunkards, nor revilers, nor robbers will inherit the kingdom of God. And such were some of you. But you were washed, you were sanctified, you were justified in the name of the Lord Jesus Christ and in the Spirit of our God. (1 Cor 6:9–11)

Paul wanted everyone to inherit the kingdom of God.[26] After enumerating several forbidden activities, he reminds his readers, "And such were some of you." The apostle focuses on the hope of his message. Through the power of God, the wrongdoer may be helped. The Holy Spirit enables the person to live a life pleasing to God. Likewise in his epistle to the Galatians, Paul speaks of activities that will exclude the individual from the kingdom of heaven:[27]

> Now the works of the flesh are plain: fornication, impurity, licentiousness, idolatry, sorcery, enmity, strife, jealousy, anger, selfishness, dissension, party spirit, envy, drunkenness, carousing, and the like. I tell you, as I warned you before, that those who do such things shall not inherit the kingdom of God. But the fruit of the Spirit is love, joy, peace, patience, kindness, goodness, faithfulness, gentleness, self-control; against such there is no law. And those who belong to Christ Jesus have crucified the flesh and its passions and desires. (Gal 5:18–24)

On the one hand, the works of the flesh force a person out of the kingdom of heaven. But the fruit of the Spirit brings hope and deliverance. Healing the inner hurt is a work of the Holy Spirit. The natural produce of the Spirit's growth in the Christian is "love, joy, peace, patience, kindness, goodness, faithfulness, gentleness, self-control." The one living in the power of the Holy Spirit will exemplify these qualities. The kingdom is always expressed in a righteous way of life. The kingdom will be revealed in greater force as God continues to act redemptively, finally culminating in the Parousia.[28]

Receiving the kingdom of heaven signifies acknowledging God's presence in every aspect of human existence and working alongside God in his effort to help people in need. The spiritual leaders of ancient Judaism sought to obey God's will as they acknowledged his divine lordship in every aspect of their daily lives. In a similar way, Jesus focuses upon God's reign as a way of life. The last verse in the book of Acts describes the Apostle Paul as "preaching the kingdom of God and teaching about the Lord Jesus Christ quite openly and unhindered." In the New Testament, Paul is last remembered as teaching everyone about the kingdom of heaven. Paul urged people to accept the power of God into their lives. He preached the kingdom as he proclaimed the meaning of Jesus' sufferings and the plan of redemption. But the Apostle Paul upheld a high moral and ethical standard in the churches he established. His ethics were based upon his training as a Pharisee and his love for Torah.

People need to experience God's power as it is demonstrated in the divine sovereignty. The kingdom of heaven is here in full force. As people experience all that God is and as they seek to obey his will, they enter into the kingdom of heaven. The kingdom comes from God alone. The concept of the divine nature is inextricably connected to God's sovereignty. God is one. He reigns in supreme authority and power. Each person created in the divine image is called to enter his great love and power as he or she seeks first and foremost God's sovereignty in every experience of life. As a Jewish theologian, a Pharisee among Jews, Christians, and pagans, the Apostle Paul called people to pursue earnestly the rule of God and his righteousness in the power of the Holy Spirit.

THE ESSENCE OF PAUL'S JEWISH FAITH: NOTES

1. Here it is not the purpose of this brief study to deal with all the theological questions related to the Christian doctrine of the Trinity, which can too easily become a form of tritheism, a heresy condemned by the church. On these important questions, see C. C. Richardson, *The Doctrine of the Trinity* (New York: Abingdon, 1958); and M. Erickson, *Christian Theology* (Grand Rapids: Baker, 1989). The eminent Christian theologian Jürgen Moltmann has discussed the doctrine with the Jewish scholar Pinchas Lapide in an important monograph, J. Moltmann and P. Lapide, *Jewish Monotheism and Christian Trinitarian Doctrine* (Philadelphia: Fortress, 1979). Today one senses the great need for a much better understanding of Jewish faith by Christians. An outstanding and challenging book that will stimulate further study is Thoma, *A Christian Theology of Judaism*.

2. See also the pioneering work of F. Mussner, *Tractate on the Jews* (Philadelphia: Fortress, 1984); and Thoma, *A Christian Theology of Judaism*. See also S. Schechter, *Studies in Judaism* (Philadelphia: Jewish Publication Society, 1896) 233–51. Many mistakes would have been avoided if Schechter's contributions were more widely known and utilized by scholars.

3. The well-known Israeli talmudic scholar Ephraim Urbach, *The Sages*, 1.19, explains, "The monotheistic concept of One God, beside whom there is no other, was at the beginning of our epoch the heritage of the whole Jewish people. . . . [T]he duty [was] to read the verse Deuteronomy vi 1 ('Hear, O Israel,' etc.) twice a day, and this very act implied the establishment of the belief in the Unity of God as the supreme creed."

4. Hertz, *Daily Prayer Book*, 116.

5. Ibid.

6. *J. Ber.* 4b, ch. 2, hal. 3; and the parallel in *m. Ber.* 2:2. I have discussed this passage in much greater detail in Young, *Jesus and His Jewish Parables*, 197f., where I have discussed the issues of date.

7. Urbach, *The Sages*, 400.

8. See Brad H. Young, *The Jewish Background to the Lord's Prayer* (Austin, Tex.: Center for Judaic-Christian Studies, 1984), 15. The parable appears in the *Mekilta de-Rabbi Ishmael* (trans. J. Lauterbach; Philadelphia: Jewish Publication Society, 1933) 2.229; cf. Horovitz, 219. See also my discussion of the kingdom of heaven in Young, *Jesus the Jewish Theologian*, 49–83.

9. It has been suggested that the expression is similar to philosophical monotheism, such as the declaration by Xenophanes, "There is one God

who is greatest among gods and men." The proclamation of ancient Israel, "the LORD our God, the LORD is one," as it is affirmed in first-century Judaism has far deeper significance that reaches beyond Greek philosophical discussions of monism and pluralism. Clearly James is closer to the Jewish theological interpretations of Deut 6:4 than to Greek philosophical theology. Cf. M. Dibelius, *James* (Hermeneia; Philadelphia: Fortress, 1964) 159. The entire question merits further research for greater clarity.

10. Matt 22:34–40; Mark 12:28–34; Luke 10:25–28. After combining the two love commandments in quoting Deut 6:4 and Lev 19:18, "Thou shalt love the LORD" and "Thou shalt love thy neighbor," Matthew's Gospel preserves the beautiful Semitism "On these two commandments depend all the law and the prophets" (Matt 22:40). The idiom *depend* is literally "hang upon," and the rabbis taught that the other commandments "hang" or "depend" upon "Thou shalt love thy neighbor as thyself" (see *Sifra* 86c). Here the lawyer is familiar with the Shema.

11. David Flusser, "Die Versuchung Jesu und ihr jüdischer Hintergrund," *Judaica* 45 (June 1989) 123. In talmudic literature, a detailed account is given of how R. Akiva gave his life for his faith. According to the Talmud, with his dying breath R. Akiva said the word "one" of the Shema. The Talmud portrays the shocking episode from Jewish history in which R. Akiva fulfilled his love for God with all his life, as he died affirming his beliefs: "It was precisely the time in which one recited the Shema and they tore his flesh from his body with iron combs. But he took the yoke of the kingdom of heaven upon him and prayed the prayer . . ." (*b. Ber.* 61b and parallels).

12. See Flusser, "Die Versuchung Jesu," 113. The addition of the word *only* seems to represent one Hebrew text type (i.e., a group of manuscripts) that circulated in the land of Israel during the time of Jesus.

13. See the treatment of the temptation of Jesus in Young, *Jesus the Jewish Theologian*, 27–34.

14. See C. K. Barrett, *A Commentary on the First Epistle to the Corinthians* (BNTC; Peabody, Mass.: Hendrickson, 1987) 193, who notes that O. Cullmann "rightly points out, the Father and the Son are distinguished not by their spheres of operation (creation and redemption) but by their propositions, *from* and *to* of the one, *through* of the other. In creation and redemption Jesus occupies a place held in Judaism by personified Wisdom and personified Law. . . . Jesus Christ is the divine agent in whose action God is perceived . . ." No doubt the strong belief in the oneness of God permeated Paul's missionary activity in a world of paganism. He seems to reflect his monotheism when he teaches on spiritual manifestations in 1 Cor 12:4–6 and stresses that all gifts proceed from the same

God. The working of the Spirit in the life of the congregation could create questions among members with a pagan background. Paul affirms the oneness of God (see also Eph 4:4; Rom 3:30; Gal 3:20; 1 Tim 2:5; also cf. Jude 20).

15. See my discussion of this text in Young, *Jesus and His Jewish Parables*, 197, 226 n. 22; also Flusser, *Judaism and the Origins of Christianity*, 652–53.

16. *M. Ber.* 2:5. It is likely, but not absolutely certain, that this is Rabban Gamaliel of Yavneh rather than Rabban the Elder, who taught Paul.

17. See Wilson, *Our Father Abraham*, 3–18.

18. See Young, *Jesus and His Jewish Parables*, 189–235.

19. See Jack Finegan, *Myth and Mystery: An Introduction to the Pagan Religions of the Biblical World* (Grand Rapids: Baker Book House, 1989); James M. Robinson, ed., *The Nag Hammadi Library* (rev. ed.; San Francisco: Harper, 1990); and Young, "The Ascension Motif."

20. See Acts 23:6–10; Josephus, *Ant.* 13.10.6 (297); 18.1.3 (12–13).

21. See Barrett, *A Commentary*, 334–85; and Fee, *The First Epistle to the Corinthians*, 713–809.

22. *B. Sanh.* 90b and parallels; cf. also Pinchas Lapide, *The Resurrection of Jesus: A Jewish Perspective* (Minneapolis: Augsburg, 1983) 61. Here we have used, with some modification, the translation in Lapide's book. Compare also the Soncino translation on *Sanh.*, 604–605.

23. See Luke 20:27–40; Matt 22:23–33; Mark 12:18–27.

24. See *b. Sanh.* 91a–b; cf. my discussion of the parallels to this fascinating rabbinic parable in Young, *Jesus and His Jewish Parables*, 64–68, 113–14.

25. See *b. Sanh.* 90b; cf. Simcha Paull Raphael, *Jewish Views of the Afterlife* (London: Jason Aronson, 1994) 156–60.

26. Cf. Heikki Räisänen, *Paul and the Law* (Philadelphia: Fortress, 1983) 68, who admits, "The law, reinterpreted to be sure, can thus be used not only as a collection of christological proof texts, but also as a *norm for behaviour.*" Fee, *The First Epistle to the Corinthians*, 716, makes a similar point: "Furthermore, all of this is integrally tied to the matters of behavior that have preceded. It is of more than passing interest that both major sections of this argument conclude with exhortation to proper behavior." Paul's pneumatology influenced his understanding of Christian conduct and moral responsibility.

27. Cf. James D. G. Dunn, *The Epistle to the Galatians* (BNTC; Peabody, Mass.: Hendrickson, 1993) 300–317. Dunn properly understands the

issue in Galatians as requiring Gentile believers to become proselytes, which is "the opposite of the inward reality of the Spirit's work" (p. 301). All Christians must be led by the Spirit. Cf. H. D. Betz, *Galatians* (Hermeneia; Philadelphia: Fortress, 1979) 271–90.

28. Cf. Paul's own words, "For as in Adam all die, so also in Christ shall all be made alive. But each in his own order: Christ the first fruits, then at his coming those who belong to Christ. Then comes the end, when he delivers the kingdom of God to the Father after destroying every rule and every authority and power" (1 Cor 15:21–24).

10 Seven Pillars of Paul's Jewish Theology

The real nearness of God as the mystery implied in being within the covenant is a truth which has never been entirely lost by the Jews in any period of their history. The kawwanah, or surrender to God, has flowered even in the thickest undergrowth of juristical debates and decisions; and the Shekinah, which means the real presence of God now, has never departed from Israel according to her faith. . . . If, however, in the last section Paul's criticism of the law has been placed in the framework of the history of the Jewish religion, and has been explained as a possible means to the renewal of the classic Judaic fear of God and a new realization of the meaning of the covenant, even though this means in fact has never been adopted, this was done because the historian of religion is concerned to do justice to every aspect of a matter. The Jews might with some justice describe the venture as the rescue of the heretic.

H. J. Schoeps
*Paul: The Theology of the Apostle in the
Light of Jewish Religious History*

SEVEN PILLARS OF PAUL'S JEWISH THEOLOGY

(1) Paul was a Pharisee. He never converted from one religion to another. The Jewish apostle to the Gentiles continued to maintain the beliefs and religious observances of the Pharisees all his life, as can be seen in his teachings on the resurrection (1 Cor 15) and circumcision (Gal 5:3).

(2) Paul's view of Torah was always positive. Torah is good. It is a spiritual revealing of God's higher plan. God's gift of Torah was an expression of divine grace. For Paul, the law and the prophets reveal the design of Jesus' coming. But the issue for Paul is human frailty and the inability of the individual to live a life for God in the strength of the flesh. Indeed, the problem of sinful flesh plagued Paul because of his intense desire to live a life pleasing to God in accordance with what had been revealed in Torah. Paul's problem is human weakness in the sinful flesh—not Torah. The individual must die to self and live for God in the vitality of Jesus' resurrection life.

(3) Paul's mission separated him from the historical Jesus. Paul and Jesus shared a common bond in their positive view of Torah (Matt 5:17; Rom 3:31), but Jesus' work among the Jewish people and Paul's missionary efforts among pagan Gentiles made each distinctive in the development of early Christianity. Paul labored to reach the pagans with the message of salvation by grace through faith in Jesus the Messiah. Jesus, on the other hand, did not minister widely to non-Jews. In preaching Jesus, Paul called the pagans to faith in God. They must abandon the worship of gods for the faith in the one true God of Israel and receive his kingdom with joy. The power of the Holy Spirit gives strength for each individual to live a life pleasing to God. The resurrection of Jesus liberates the believer from the power of sin in the flesh in order to live a life of righteousness in obedience to God. The Gentile must not pretend to be Jewish by keeping all the ceremonial laws in Torah. The Jewish believer must not behave like a Gentile, disregarding his or her rich heritage.

(4) Healing love must characterize the Christian's life of ministry to others. God's presence is experienced through the Holy Spirit's empowerment to bring healing and help to people in need.

(5) The grace of God is revealed through Jesus the Messiah. The people involved in sinful activity will not inherit the kingdom of God. But all may be forgiven and restored to fellowship with God.

(6) The resurrection of Jesus is the first fruit. In the bodily resurrection, God will reconcile the physical material world with the spiritual dimension of the divine presence. By dying to selfish wants and desires, the believer must walk in the resurrection power in order to live a holy life.

(7) Jesus is coming again to complete the work of redemption. All must be prepared for the day of judgment. God has not rejected his people Israel. Paul taught the engraftment of the non-Jewish Christian believers and not the church's replacement of the physical people of Israel.[1] While many Jewish people received Paul's message about Jesus, the majority did not. But those Israelites who rejected Jesus have performed a great service to the pagan Gentiles. By saying "no" to Jesus, they are seeking in their own understanding to say "yes" to the God of Israel and his covenants. Their "no" to Jesus has made it possible for the pagan Gentiles to receive the message of Jesus and experience the power of God. The Gentiles have been grafted into the olive tree. The higher redemptive purpose of all time, however, concerns both Jew and non-Jew in the plan of salvation.[2] The Christian church must reject the path of arrogance concerning God's people the Jews. Christians must stand in awe at the mystery of God and walk in love with their brothers and sisters dedicated to Jewish faith and practice. God's family is larger than finite human conceptions. Paul is not ashamed of the gospel that he preaches as the power of God to both Jew and Gentile in the mysterious plan of God. Even now the kingdom comes, not in word only but in power, to bring healing and wholeness to a world in need.

SEVEN PILLARS OF PAUL'S JEWISH THEOLOGY: NOTES

1. Cf. Leon Klenicki, "From Argument to Dialogue," in *Biblical Studies: Meeting Ground of Jews and Christians* (ed. Lawrence Boadt, Helga Croner, and Leon Klenicki; New York: Paulist, 1980) 191: "Israel, God's chosen, existed and exists, witnessing God and the covenantal relation-

ship, despite alienation and ostracism which culminated in the Holocaust, a devastating reality of total evil. The Holocaust reminds Christians and Jews of the historical necessity to recognize that direct and indirect involvement of Christians in the cultural milieu of the Western world made possible antisemitism in its most extreme manifestation."

2. Cf. the discussion of Romans 9, 10, and 11 by Ladd, *A Commentary on the Revelation of John*, 150–51: "It is difficult to interpret these three chapters symbolically of the church—the spiritual Israel. They teach that literal Israel is yet to be included in spiritual Israel. . . . Our Lord himself had anticipated this. After his lament over Jerusalem, he asserted, 'For I tell you, you will not see me again, until you say, "Blessed be he who comes in the name of the Lord" '(Matt 23:39). Again, he implied the salvation of Israel when he said, 'Jerusalem will be trodden down by the Gentiles *until* the times of the Gentiles are fulfilled' (Luke 21:24). We believe with such scholars as I. T. Beckwith, W. H. Simcox, and Theodor Zahn that the prophecy in Revelation 11 is John's way of predicting the preservation of the Jewish people and their final salvation." Does God break covenant with one to fulfill a promise with another? Paul describes the redemptive acts of God surrounding Jesus as a mystery with a present reality and a future fulfillment. By using the word *mystery,* Paul indicates that much is left in the hands of God. The apostle does not claim to fully understand this mystery but believes in God's faithfulness and sovereignty.

BIBLIOGRAPHY

Primary Sources, Editions, and Translations

Amidon, P. *The Panarion of St. Epiphanius.* Oxford: Clarendon, 1990.

Avot de Rabbi Natan. Edited by S. Schechter. Vienna: Ch. Lippe, 1887.

Black, M. *The Book of Enoch.* Leiden: Brill, 1985.

Braude, W. G. *The Midrash on Psalms.* 2 vols. New Haven: Yale University Press, 1958.

_____. *Pesikta Rabbati.* 2 vols. New Haven: Yale University Press, 1968.

_____. *Pesikta-de-Rab-Kahana.* Philadelphia: The Jewish Publication Society, 1975.

_____. *Tanna Debe Eliyyahu.* Philadelphia: The Jewish Publication Society, 1981.

Charles, R. H., ed. *The Apocrypha and Pseudepigrapha of the Old Testament.* 2 vols. Oxford: Clarendon, 1977.

Charles, R. H., trans. and ed. *The Book of Jubilees.* London: A. & C. Black, 1902.

Charlesworth, J. H., ed. *The Old Testament Pseudepigrapha.* 2 vols. New York: Doubleday, 1983.

Clark, E. G. *Targum Pseudo-Jonathan of the Pentateuch.* Hoboken, N.J.: Ktav, 1984.

Cohen, A., and Israel Brodie, eds. *The Minor Tractates of the Talmud.* 2 vols. London: Soncino, 1971.

Danby, Herbert. *The Mishnah.* New York: Oxford, 1977.

The Dead Sea Scrolls on Microfiche. Edited by E. Tov. Leiden: Brill, 1993.

Díez Macho, A. *Neophyti I.* 6 vols. Text and translations into Spanish, French, and English. Madrid: Consejo Superior de Investigaciones Cientficas, 1968–79.

Dupont-Sommer, A. *The Essene Writings from Qumran.* Gloucester, Mass.: Peter Smith, 1973.

Elliot, J. K. *The Apocryphal New Testament.* Oxford: Clarendon, 1993.

Epstein, I., ed. *The Babylonian Talmud.* 35 vols. London: Soncino, 1935–78.

Freedman, H., ed. *Midrash Rabbah.* 9 vols. London: Soncino, 1951.

Friedlander, G. *Pirke de Rabbi Eliezer.* New York: Hermon, 1981.

Gaster, T. *The Dead Sea Scriptures.* New York: Anchor, 1976.

Goldin, J. *The Fathers according to Rabbi Nathan.* New York: Schocken, 1974.

Haberman, A. *Megillot Midbar Yehuda.* Tel Aviv, Israel: Machbarot Lesifrut, 1959.

Hammer, Reuven, *Sifre: A Tannaitic Commentary on the Book of Deuteronomy.* New Haven: Yale University Press, 1986.

Hertz, J. H. *The Authorised Daily Prayer Book* (Hebrew text, English translation with commentary and notes). New York: Bloch, 1959.

Herford, T. *Pirke Aboth: The Ethics of the Talmud: Sayings of the Fathers.* New York: Schocken, 1975.

James, M. R. *The Apocryphal New Testament.* Oxford: Clarendon, 1980.

Josephus. 9 vols. Edited and translated by H. J. Thackeray. Cambridge: Harvard University Press, 1978.

Klein, M. L. *The Fragment-Targums of the Pentateuch.* 2 vols. Rome: Pontifical Biblical Institute Press, 1980.

Masechet Semachot. Edited by M. Higger. Jerusalem: Makor, 1970.

Masechtot Derech Eretz. 2 vols. Hebrew text and English translation. Edited by M. Higger. Makor: Jerusalem, 1970.

Mekilta Derabbi Ishmael. Edited by H. S. Horovitz and Ch. Rabin. Jerusalem: Wahrmann Books, 1970.

Mekilta Derabbi Ishmael. Edited by M. Friedmann. 1870. Reprint. Jerusalem: Old City Press, 1978.

Mekilta Derabbi Ishmael. 3 vols. Edited and translated by Jacob Lauterbach. Philadelphia: Jewish Publication Society, 1976.

Mekilta Derabbi Shimeon Bar Yochai. Edited by Y. N. Epstein and E. Z. Melamed. Jerusalem: Hillel, 1980.

Midrash Bereshit Rabbah. 3 vols. Edited by Ch. Albeck and J. Theodor. Jerusalem: Wahrmann Books, 1980.

Midrash Devarim Rabbah. Edited by S. Liebermann. Jerusalem: Wahrmann Books, 1974.

Midrash Echa Rabbah. Edited by S. Buber. Wilna: Wittwa & Gebrüder Romm, 1899.

Midrash Hagadol. 5 vols. Jerusalem: Mosad Harav Kook, 1975.

Midrash Lekach Tov. Edited by S. Buber. Wilna: Wittwa & Gebrüder Romm, 1880.

Midrash Mishle. Edited by S. Buber. Wilna: Wittwa & Gebrüder Romm, 1891.

Midrash Rabbah. 11 vols., on the Torah. Edited and with commentary by Moshe Mirkin. Tel Aviv: Yavneh, 1977.

Midrash Rabbah. 2 vols. Wilna: Wittwa & Gebrüder Romm, 1887.

Midrash Rut Rabbah. Edited by M. Lerner. Ph.D. diss., Hebrew University, 1971.

Midrash Seder Olam. Edited by D. Ratner. New York: Talmudic Research Institute, 1966.

Midrash Shemuel. Edited by S. Buber. Krakau: Joseph Fischer, 1893.

Midrash Shir Hashirim. Edited by Eliezer Halevi Grunhut. Jerusalem, 1897.

Midrash Shir Hashirim Rabbah. Edited by Shimshon Donski. Tel Aviv: Dvir, 1980.

Midrash Tanchuma. Edited by S. Buber. Wilna: Wittwa & Gebrüder Romm, 1885.

Midrash Tanchuma. 1879. Reprint. Jerusalem: Lewin-Epstein, 1975.

Midrash Tannaim. Edited by D. Hoffmann. 1908. Reprint. Jerusalem: Books Export, n.d.

Midrash Tehilim. Edited by S. Buber. Wilna: Wittwa & Gebrüder Romm, 1891.

Midrash Vayikra Rabbah. 5 vols. Edited by M. Margulies. Jerusalem: Wahrmann Books, 1970.

Mishnah. 6 vols. Edited by Ch. Albeck. Jerusalem: Bialik Institute, 1978.

The New Testament in Greek: The Gospel according to St. Luke. 2 vols. Edited by the American and British Committees of the International Greek New Testament Project. Oxford: Clarendon, 1984–87.

Nitzan, Bilha. *Pesher Habakkuk: A Scroll from the Wilderness of Judaea (1QpHab).* Jerusalem: Bialik, 1986.

Novum Testamentum Graece. 2 vols. Edited by S. C. E. Legg. Oxford: Clarendon, 1935–40.

Pesikta Derav Kahana. Edited by B. Mandelbaum. New York: Jewish Theological Seminary, 1962.

Pesikta Derav Kahana. Edited by S. Buber. Lyck: L. Silbermann, 1868.

Pesikta Rabbati. Edited by M. Friedmann. Vienna: Josef Kaiser, 1880.

Philo. 10 vols. and 2 supp. vols. Edited and translated by F. H. Colson and G. H. Whitaker. Cambridge: Harvard University Press, 1981.

Roberts, A., and J. Donaldson. *The Ante-Nicene Fathers.* Peabody: Hendrickson, 1994.

Pirke Derabbi Eliezer. Edited by David Luria. Warsaw: Bomberg, 1852.

Seder Eliyahu Rabbah. Edited by M. Friedmann. Jerusalem: Wahrmann Books, 1969.

Sifra: An Analytical Translation. 3 vols. Translated by J. Neusner. Atlanta: Scholars Press, 1985.

Sifra. Edited by J. H. Weiss. Vienna, 1862.

Sifra. 5 vols. Edited by L. Finkelstein. New York: The Jewish Theological Seminary of America, 1984.

Sifra (incomplete). Edited by M. Friedmann. 1915. Reprint. Jerusalem: Old City Press, 1978.

Sifre Al Bemidbar Vesifre Zuta. Edited by H. S. Horovitz. Jerusalem: Wahrmann Books, 1966.

Sifre Debe Rav. Edited by M. Friedmann. 1864. Reprint. Jerusalem: Old City Press, 1978.

Sifre Devarim. Edited by L. Finkelstein. New York: The Jewish Theological Seminary of America, 1969.

Sifre to Numbers. 3 vols. Translated by J. Neusner. Atlanta: Scholars Press, 1986.

Sperber, A. *The Bible in Aramaic.* 5 vols. Leiden: Brill, 1959–68.

Taylor, C. *Sayings of the Fathers.* 2 vols. Cambridge: Cambridge University Press, 1877.

Talmud Babli. Wilna: Wittwa & Gebrüder Romm, 1835.

Talmud Jerushalmi. Krotoshin: Dov Baer Monash, 1866.

Torah Shelemah. 43 vols. Edited by M. Kasher. New York and Jerusalem: Talmud Institute, 1951–83.

Tosefta. Edited by M. Zuckermandel. Jerusalem: Wahrmann Books, 1937.

Tosefta. 15 vols. Edited with commentary by S. Liebermann. New York: Jewish Theological Seminary of America, 1955–77.

Visotzky, Burton. *Midrash Mishle.* New York: Jewish Theological Seminary of America, 1990.

Vermes, G. *The Dead Sea Scrolls in English.* Baltimore: Penguin Books, 1988.

Wacholder, B. and M. Abegg. *A Preliminary Edition of the Unpublished Dead Sea Scrolls.* Washington D.C.: Biblical Archaeological Society, 1991–92.

Wise, M., M. Abegg, and E. Cook. *The Dead Sea Scrolls.* San Francisco: HarperSanFrancisco, 1996.

Yalkut Hamakiri. Edited by A. W. Greenup. Jerusalem: Hameitar, 1968.

Yalkut Hamakiri. Edited by S. Buber. Berdichev: Ch. J. Schefftel, 1899.

Yalkut Hamakiri. Edited by J. Z. Kahana-Shapira. 1893. Reprint. Jerusalem: Zvi Hirsch, 1964.

Yalkut Shimoni. Wilna: Wittwa & Gebrüder Romm, 1898.

Grammars and Lexical Aids

Arndt, W., and F. W. Gingrich. *A Greek-English Lexicon of the New Testament and Other Early Christian Literature.* Chicago: Chicago University Press, 1979.

Blass, F., and A. Debrunner. *A Greek Grammar of the New Testament.* Translated and revised by R. Funk. Chicago: Chicago University Press, 1961.

Brown, F. *The New Brown-Driver-Briggs-Gesenius Hebrew and English Lexicon.* Peabody, Mass.: Hendrickson, 1979.

Dalman, G. *Aramäisch-neuhebräisches Handwörterbuch.* Frankfurt am Main: J. Kaufmann, 1922.

_____. *Grammatik die jüdisch-palästinischen Aramäisch.* Leipzig: J. C. Hinrich, 1905.

Jastrow, M. *A Dictionary of the Targumim, the Talmud Babli and Yerushalmi, and the Midrashic Literature.* 2 vols. Reprint. New York: Judaica Press, 1975.

Kasovsky, Ch. *Otzar Leshon Hamishnah.* Tel Aviv: Masadah Publishing Company, 1967.

Kittel, G. *Theological Dictionary of the New Testament.* Translated by G. Bromiley. Grand Rapids: Eerdmans, 1983.

_____. *Otzar Leshon Hatalmud.* Jerusalem: Ministry of Education and Culture, Government of Israel, 1971.

_____. *Otzar Leshon Hatosefta.* New York: The Jewish Theological Seminary of America, 1961.

Kosovsky, M. *Otzar Leshon Talmud Yerushalmi* (incomplete). Jerusalem: Israel Academy of Sciences and Humanities, 1979.

Levy, J. *Wörterbuch über die Talmudim und Midraschim.* 4 vols. Berlin: Benjamin Harz, 1924.

Liddell, H. G., and R. Scott, *A Greek-English Lexicon.* Oxford: Clarendon, 1976.

Moulton, J. H. *A Grammar of New Testament Greek.* 4 vols. Edinburgh: T. & T. Clark, 1978.

Stevenson, W. B. *Grammar of Palestinian Jewish Aramaic.* Oxford: Oxford University Press, 1974.

General Sources and Study Aids

Abbott, Edwin. *Clue a Guide through Greek to Hebrew Scripture.* London: Adam and Charles Black, 1900.

Abrahams, Israel. *Studies in Pharisaism and the Gospels.* New York: Ktav, 1967.

Aland, Kurt, and Barbara Aland. *The Text of the New Testament.* Grand Rapids: Eerdmans, 1989.

Albright, W. F., and C. S. Mann. *The Gospel according to Matthew.* AB. *New York: Doubleday, 1981.*

Avigad, N. *Discovering Jerusalem.* Jerusalem: Israel Exploration Society, 1980.

Avi–Yonah, Michael, *Views of the Biblical World.* 5 vols. Jerusalem: International Publishing, 1961.

Ayali, M. *Poalim Veomanim.* Jerusalem: Yad Letalmud, 1987.

Bacher, W. *Die Agada der palästinensischen Amoräer.* Strassburg: Karl Trübner, 1892–99. Translated into Hebrew by A. Rabinovitz. *Agadot Amore Eretz Israel.* Jerusalem: Davir, 1926.

_____. *Die Agada der Tannaiten.* Strassburg: Karl Trübner, 1890. Translated into Hebrew by A. Rabinovitz. *Agadot Hatannaim.* Jerusalem: Davir, 1919.

_____. *Die exegetische Terminologie der jüdischen Traditionsliteratur.* Leipzig: J. C. Hinrich, 1905. Translated into Hebrew by A. Rabinovitz. *Erche Midrash.* Jerusalem: Carmiel, 1970.

Bacher, W. *Tradition und Tradenten.* Leipzig: Gustav Fock, 1914.

Baeck, Leo. *Judaism and Christianity.* New York: Leo Baeck Institute, 1958.

Bailey, Kenneth E. *Poet & Peasant.* Grand Rapids: Eerdmans, 1976.

_____. *Through Peasant Eyes.* Grand Rapids: Eerdmans, 1980.

Baarda, T. A., G. Hilhorst, P. Luttikhuizen, and A. S. van der Woude, eds. *Text and Testimony.* Kampen: J. H. Kok, 1988.

Barth, M. *Ephesians.* Garden City: Doubleday, 1982.

Barrett, C. K. *A Commentary on the First Epistle to the Corinthians.* Peabody, Mass.: Hendrickson, 1987.

_____. *Essays on Paul.* Philadelphia: Westminster, 1982.

Bauernfeind, Otto. *Kommentar und Studien zur Apostelgeschichte.* Tübingen: J. C. B. Mohr, 1980.

Beall, Todd. *Josephus' Description of the Essenes Illustrated by the Dead Sea Scrolls.* Cambridge: Cambridge University Press, 1988.

Beasley-Murray, G. R. *Jesus and the Kingdom of God.* Grand Rapids: Eerdmans, 1987.

Beker, Christian. *Paul the Apostle: The Triumph of God in Life and Thought*. Philadelphia: Fortress, 1980.

Ben Dov, Meir. *In the Shadow of the Temple*. Jerusalem: Keter, 1982.

Bengel, J. A. *Gnomon of the New Testament*. Philadelphia: Perkinpine & Higgins, 1860.

Benoit, P. "Qumran and the New Testament." In *Paul and the Dead Sea Scrolls*. Edited by J. Murphy O'Connor and J. Charlesworth. New York: Crossroad, 1990.

Ben-Yehuda, Eliezer. *Complete Dictionary of Ancient and Modern Hebrew*. 17 vols. Tel Aviv: La'am Publishing Company, 1959.

Betz, H. D. *Galatians*. Philadelphia: Fortress, 1979.

Billerbeck, P. *Kommentar zum Neuen Testament aus Talmud und Midrasch*. 6 vols. Munich: C. H. Beck, 1978.

Birdsall, J. N. "The New Testament Text." In *Cambridge History of the Bible*. Cambridge: Cambridge University Press, 1963–70. 1.308–77.

Bivin, David, and Roy Blizzard. *Understanding the Difficult Words of Jesus*. Arcadia: Makor Foundation, 1983.

Black, M. *An Aramaic Approach to the Gospels and Acts*. Oxford: Clarendon, 1977.

Blackman, E. C. *Marcion and His Influence*. London: SPCK, 1948.

Blizzard, Roy B., Jr. *Let Judah Go Up First*. Austin: Center for Judaic-Christian Studies, 1984.

Boers, Hendrikus. "The Problem of Jews and Gentiles in the Macro-Structure of Romans." *Svensk exegetisk årsbok* 47 (1982), 184–96.

Boismard, M., and A. Lamouille. *Synopsis Graeca Quattuor Evangeliorum*. Paris: Peeters, 1986.

Brown, R., *The Birth of the Messiah*. New York: Doubleday, 1977.

_____. *The Death of the Messiah*. Mahwah: Paulist, 1994.

_____. *New Testament Essays*. Milwaukee: Bruce, 1965.

Brown, R., and J. Meier. *Antioch and Jerusalem*. New York: Paulist, 1983.

Bruce, F. F. *The Acts of the Apostles*. Grand Rapids: Eerdmans, 1984.

_____. *Paul*. Grand Rapids: Eerdmans, 1977.

Buber, Martin. *Two Types of Faith*. New York: Macmillan, 1961.

Büchler, Adolf. *Types of Jewish-Palestinian Peity*. London: Jews' College, 1922.

Bultmann, Rudolf. *History of the Synoptic Tradition*. 1963. Reprint. Peabody, Mass.: Hendrickson, 1993.

_____. *Theology of the New Testament*. London: SCM, 1952.

Buxbaum, Yitzhak. *The Life and Teachings of Hillel.* London: Jason Aronson, 1994.

Chajes, Z. H. *The Student's Guide through the Talmud.* Translated by J. Schachter. New York: Feldheim, 1960.

Charlesworth, James H., ed. *Messiah.* Minneapolis: Fortress, 1992.

Cohen, B. *Everyman's Talmud.* New York: Schocken Books, 1975.

Cohn, Haim. *The Trial and Death of Jesus.* New York: KTAV, 1977.

Conzelmann, H. *1 Corinthians.* Philadelphia: Fortress, 1975.

Dalman, G. *The Words of Jesus.* Edinburgh: T. & T. Clark, 1909.

_____. *Jesus-Jeshua.* London: SPCK, 1929.

_____. *Sacred Sites and Sacred Ways.* London: SPCK, 1935.

Daniélou, Jean. *The Bible and the Liturgy.* Indiana: University of Notre Dame Press, 1956.

_____. *The Theology of Jewish-Christianity.* London: Darton, Longman & Todd, 1964.

Daube, David. *The New Testament and Rabbinic Judaism.* New York: Arno, 1973.

Davies, W. D., and D. Allison. *The Gospel according to St. Matthew.* ICC. Edinburgh: T. & T. Clark, 1988–91.

Davies, W. D. *Jewish and Pauline Studies.* Philadelphia: Fortress, 1984.

_____. *Paul and Rabbinic Judaism.* London: SPCK, 1980.

_____. *The Setting of the Sermon on the Mount.* Atlanta: Scholars Press, 1989.

Dibelius, M. *James.* Philadelphia: Fortress, 1964.

Dodd, C. H. *The Parables of the Kingdom.* Glasgow: Collins, 1961.

Donaldson, Terence L. *Paul and the Gentiles.* Minneapolis: Fortress, 1997.

Doeve, J. W. *Jewish Hermeneutics in the Synoptic Gospels and Acts.* Assen: Van Gorcum, 1954.

Dunn, James D. G. *The Epistle to the Galatians.* Peabody, Mass.: Hendrickson, 1993.

_____. *Romans.* Dallas: Word, 1988.

Elbogen, I. *Jewish Liturgy.* Philadelphia: Jewish Publication Society, 1993.

Encyclopaedia Judaica. Jerusalem: Keter, 1978.

Ellis, E. E. *Pauline Theology.* Grand Rapids: Eerdmans, 1989.

Erickson, M. *Christian Theology.* Grand Rapids: Baker, 1989.

Fee, Gordon D. *The First Epistle to the Corinthians.* Grand Rapids: Eerdmans, 1987.

Foakes Jackson, F. J., and Kirsopp Lake. *The Beginnings of Christianity.* Grand Rapids: Baker, 1979.

Finegan, Jack. *Myth and Mystery: An Introduction to the Pagan Religions of the Biblical World.* Grand Rapids: Baker, 1989.

Fitzmyer, J. A. *The Gospel according to Luke.* New York: Doubleday, 1981.

———. *Pauline Theology: A Brief Sketch.* Englewood Cliffs: Prentice-Hall, 1967.

———. *Romans: A New Translation with Introduction and Commentary.* AB. New York: Doubleday, 1993.

———. *A Wandering Aramean.* Chico: Scholars Press, 1979.

Finkelstein, L. *The Pharisees.* Philadelphia: Jewish Publication Society, 1962.

Flusser, David. "Blessed are the Poor in Spirit." *Israel Exploration Journal* 10 (1960).

———. "The Dead Sea Scrolls and Pre-Pauline Christianity." In *Judaism and the Origins of Christianity.* Jerusalem: Magnes, 1988. Pages 23–74.

———. *Jesus in Selbstzeugnissen und Bilddokumenten.* Hamburg: Rowohlt, 1968 (a poor translation into English was published; New York: Herder & Herder, 1969).

———. *Jewish Sources in Early Christianity.* Tel Aviv: MOD Books, 1989.

———. *Judaism and the Origins of Christianity.* Jerusalem: Magnes, 1989.

———. "Paul's Jewish-Christian Opponents in the Didache." In *Gilgul: Essays on Transformation, Revolution and Permanence in the History of Religions. Dedicated to R. J. Zwi Werblowski.* Edited by S. Shaked, D. Shulman, and G. G. Strumsa. Leiden: Brill, 1987. Pages 71–90.

———. "Paulinism in Paul." In *Yahadut Umekorot Hanatzrut.* Tel Aviv: Sifriyat Hapoalim, 1979. Pages 359–80 (Hebrew).

———. *Die rabbinischen Gleichnisse und der Gleichniserzähler Jesus.* Bern: Peter Lang, 1981.

———. "Sanktus und Gloria." In *Abraham unser Vater: Festschrift für Otto Michel zum 60. Geburtstag.* Edited by O. Betz, M. Hengel, and P. Schmidt. Leiden: Brill, 1963.

———. "Some of the Precepts of the Torah from Qumran (4QMMT) and the Benediction against the Heretics." *Tarbitz* 61 (1992), 333–74.

———. "Some Notes to the Beatitudes." *Immanuel* 8 (Spring, 1978).

———. "Die Versuchung Jesu und ihr jüdische Hintergrund." *Judaica* 45 (1989), 110–28.

Flusser, David, and S. Safrai. "Das Aposteldekret und die Noachitis-chen Gebote." In *"Wer Tora vermehrt, mehrt Leben": Festgabe für Heinz Kremers zum 60. Geburtstag.* Edited by E. Brocke and H. J. Barkenings. Vluyn: Neukirchen, 1986. Pages 173–92.

Gaston, Loyd. *Paul and the Torah.* Vancouver: University of British Columbia Press, 1987.

Gerhardsson, Birger. *The Testing of God's Son.* Lund, Sweden: Gleerup, 1966.

Georgi, Dieter. *The Opponents of Paul in Second Corinthians.* Philadel-phia: Fortress, 1986.

Gilat, Y. R. *Eliezer ben Hyrcanus: A Scholar Outcast.* Ramat Gan, Israel: Bar Ilan University Press, 1984.

Gilmore, A. *Christian Baptism.* London: Lutterworth, 1959.

Glatzer, Nahum. *Hillel the Elder: The Emergence of Classical Judaism.* New York: B'nai B'rith Hillel Foundations, 1956.

Gnilka, J. *Der Epheserbrief.* Freiburg: Herder, 1982.

Greenberg, Irving. *The Jewish Way: Living the Holidays.* New York: Simon & Schuster, 1988.

Gros, M. *Otzar Haagadah.* 3 vols. Jerusalem: Harav Kook, 1977.

Grudem, Wayne A. *The Gift of Prophecy in 1 Corinthians.* New York: University Press of America, 1982.

Hafemann, Scott J. *Paul, Moses, and the History of Israel.* Peabody, Mass.: Hendrickson, 1996.

Harnack, Adolf von. *Marcion das Evangelium vom fremden Gott.* 1924. Reprint. Darmstadt: Wissenschaftliche Buchgesellschaft, 1985.

Harrington, D. *The Gospel of Matthew.* Collegeville, Minnesota: Mi-chael Glazier Books, 1991.

Hengel, Martin. *Judaism and Hellenism.* London: SCM, 1974.

_____. *The Pre-Christian Paul.* Philadelphia: Trinity Press Interna-tional, 1991.

_____. *Studies in the Gospel of Mark.* London: SCM, 1985.

_____. *The Zealots.* Edinburgh: T. & T. Clark, 1989.

Heschel, Abraham Joshua. *God in Search of Man.* New York: Farrar, Straus & Giroux, 1994.

_____. *The Insecurity of Freedom.* New York: Schocken, 1972.

_____. *The Prophets.* New York: Harper & Row, 1962.

_____. *Torah Men Hashamayim.* 3 vols. New York: Soncino, 1972–90.

Horbury, W. "The Messianic Associations of 'the Son of Man.' " *Journal of Theological Studies* 36 (1985), 35–55.

Howard, George. "Christ the End of the Law: the Meaning of Romans 10:4ff." *Journal of Biblical Literature* 88 (1969), 331–37.

Huck, Albert. *Synopse der drei ersten Evangelien.* Revised by Heinrich Greeven. Tübingen: J. C. B. Mohr, 1981.

Hyman, A. *Toldoth Tannaim Veamoraim.* 3 vols. Jerusalem: Boys Town Publishers, 1963.

_____. *Torah Haketubah Vehamasurah.* 3 vols. Tel Aviv: Dvir, 1979.

Jeremias, J. *Jerusalem in the Time of Jesus.* London: SCM, 1969.

_____. *The Central Message of the New Testament.* London: SCM, 1965.

_____. *New Testament Theology.* New York: Scribner, 1971.

_____. *The Parables of Jesus.* London: SCM Press, 1972.

_____. *The Prayers of Jesus.* Philadelphia: Fortress, 1984.

Jonsson, Jakob. *Humour and Irony in the New Testament.* Leiden: Brill, 1985.

Kadushin, Max. *A Conceptual Approach to the Mekilta.* New York: The Jewish Theological Seminary, [1969].

_____. *The Rabbinic Mind.* New York: Bloch, 1972.

_____. *The Theology of Seder Eliahu a Study in Organic Thinking.* New York: Bloch, 1932.

Kaylor, R. David. *Paul's Covenant Community: Jew and Gentile in Romans.* Atlanta: John Knox, 1988.

Kensky, A. "Moses and Jesus: The Birth of a Savior." *Judaism* 42 (1993), 43–49.

Kenyon, Frederic. *Handbook to the Textual Criticism of the New Testament.* London: Macmillan, 1912.

Kister, M. "Plucking on the Sabbath and Jewish-Christian Polemic." *Immanuel* 24/25 (1990), 35–51.

Klausner, Joseph. *From Jesus to Paul.* London: George Allen & Unwin Ltd., 1946.

_____. *Jesus of Nazareth.* New York: Macmillan, 1945.

_____. *The Messianic Idea in Israel.* New York: Macmillan, 1955.

Klenicki, Leon. "From Argument to Dialogue." In *Biblical Studies: Meeting Ground of Jews and Christians.* Edited by Lawrence Boadt, Helga Croner, and Leon Klenicki. New York: Paulist Press, 1980.

Kosovsky, B. *Otzar Leshon Hatannaim Lemekilta Derabbi Ishmael.* New York: Jewish Theological Seminary, 1965.

_____. *Otzar Leshon Hatannaim Lasifra.* New York: Jewish Theological Seminary, 1967.

_____. *Otzar Leshon Hatannaim Lasifre Bemidbar Vedevarim.* New York: Jewish Theological Seminary, 1971.

Lachs, S. T. *A Rabbinic Commentary on the New Testament.* Hoboken: Ktav, 1987.

Ladd, George Eldon. *A Commentary on the Revelation of John.* Grand Rapids: Eerdmans, 1993.

_____. *The Presence of the Future.* Grand Rapids: Eerdmans, 1980.

_____. *A Theology of the New Testament.* Grand Rapids: Eerdmans, 1974.

Lapide, P. *The Resurrection of Jesus: A Jewish Perspective.* Minneapolis: Augsburg, 1983.

Lapide, P., and Ulrich Luz. *Jesus in Two Perspectives.* Minneapolis: Augsburg, 1971.

Lauterbach, J. *Rabbinic Essays.* Cincinnati: Hebrew Union College Press, 1951.

_____. *The Sermon on the Mount.* New York: Orbis, 1986.

Leif, Immanuel. *"Aspaklarya." Sefer Hayovel Leprofesor Shmuel Kraus.* Jerusalem: Rubin Mass, 1936.

Levey, S. *The Messiah: An Aramaic Interpretation.* Hoboken, New Jersey: Ktav, 1974.

Levine, Lee. *Ancient Synagogues Revealed.* Jerusalem: Israel Exploration Society, 1981.

_____. *The Galilee in Late Antiquity.* New York: Jewish Theological Seminary, 1992.

Lieberman, S. *Hellenism in Jewish Palestine.* New York: Jewish Theological Seminary, 1962.

Lindsey, Robert L. *A Comparative Greek Concordance of the Synoptic Gospels.* 3 vols. Jerusalem: Baptist House, 1985–89.

_____. *A Hebrew Translation of the Gospel of Mark.* Jerusalem: Baptist House, 1973.

_____. *Jesus: Rabbi and Lord.* Oak Creek: Cornerstone, 1990.

_____. *The Jesus Sources.* Tulsa: HaKesher, 1990.

Lodahl, Michael. *The Shekhinah/Spirit Divine Presence in Jewish and Christian Religion.* New York: Paulist, 1992.

Lüdemann, Gerd. *Early Christianity according to the Traditions in Acts.* Minneapolis: Fortress, 1987.

_____. *Opposition to Paul in Jewish Christianity.* Minneapolis: Fortress, 1989.

Lundström, G. *The Kingdom of God in the Teachings of Jesus.* Richmond: John Knox, 1963.

Mackin, T. *Divorce and Remarriage.* Mahwah, N.J.: Paulist, 1984.

Malherbe, Abraham J. *Paul and the Popular Philosophers.* Minneapolis: Fortress, 1989.

Mann, C. S. *The Gospel according to Mark.* AB. New York: Doubleday, 1986.

Mann, Jacob, "Jesus and the Sadducean Priests: Luke 10:25–37." *Jewish Quarterly Review* 6 (1914), 415–22.

Marshall, I. Howard. *The Gospel of Luke*. Grand Rapids: Eerdmans, 1978.

Marrow, Stanley B. *Paul: His Letters and His Theology*. Mahwah: Paulist, 1986.

McArthur, H., and R. Johnston. *They Also Taught in Parables*. Grand Rapids: Zondervan, 1990.

McGinley, L. *Form-Criticism of the Synoptic Healing Narratives*. Woodstock: Woodstock College Press, 1944.

McNamara, M. *Targum and Testament*. Grand Rapids: Eerdmans, 1968.

M'Neile, A. H. *The Gospel according to St. Matthew*. London: Macmillan, 1949.

McRay, John. *Archaeology and the New Testament*. Grand Rapids: Baker, 1991.

Metzger, Bruce. *The Text of the New Testament: Its Transmission, Corruption, and Restoration*. New York: Oxford, 1992.

_____. *A Textual Commentary on the Greek New Testament*. New York: United Bible Societies, 1975.

Moore, G. F. "Christian Writers on Judaism." *Harvard Theological Review* 14 (1921), 197–254.

_____. *Judaism in the First Centuries of the Christian Era*. New York: Schocken, 1975.

Montefiore, C. G. *Rabbinic Literature and Gospel Teachings*. New York: Ktav, 1970.

Montefiore, C. G., and H. Loewe. *A Rabbinic Anthology*. New York: Schocken, 1974.

Montefiore, C. G. *The Synoptic Gospels*. 2 vols. New York: Ktav, 1968.

Mowinckel, Sigmund. *He That Cometh*. New York: Abingdon, 1954.

Murphy O'Connor, J. *St. Paul's Corinth Texts and Archaeology*. Collegeville, Minn.: Liturgical, 1983.

Murphy O'Connor, J., and J. Charlesworth. *Paul and the Dead Sea Scrolls*. New York: Crossroad, 1990.

Mussner, F. *Tractate on the Jews*. Philadelphia: Fortress, 1984.

Nanos, Mark D. *The Mystery of Romans*. Minneapolis: Fortress, 1996.

Nathan ben Jehiel. *Aruch Completum*. Edited by A. Kohut. Vienna: Menora, 1926.

Newman, L., and S. Spitz. *The Talmudic Anthology*. New York: Behrman House, 1945.

Notley, Richard Steven. "The Concept of the Holy Spirit in Jewish Literature of the Second Temple Period and 'Pre-Pauline' Christianity." Ph.D. diss. Hebrew University, 1991.

Qimron, Elisha, and John Strugnell. *Qumran Cave 4: Miqsat Ma'ase ha-Torah.* Oxford: Clarendon, 1994.

_____. "An Unpublished Halakhic Letter from Qumran." *Biblical Archaeology Today* (Jerusalem, 1985), 400–407.

Quasten, Johannes. *Patrology.* Westminster, Md.: Christian Classics, 1988.

Raphael, Simcha Paull. *Jewish Views of the Afterlife.* London: Jason Aronson, 1994.

Räisänen, Heikki. *Paul and the Law.* Philadelphia: Fortress, 1983.

Resch, A. "Das Aposteldekret nach seiner ausserkanonischen Textgestalt untersucht." *Texte und Untersuchungen,* NF, Bd. 3 (Leipzig, 1905), 1–179.

Reumann, John. *Righteousness in the New Testament.* Mahwah: Paulist, 1982.

Ridderbos, Herman. *Paul: An Outline of His Theology.* Grand Rapids: Eerdmans, 1975.

Robinson, James M., gen. ed. *The Nag Hammadi Library.* Rev. ed. San Francisco: Harper, 1990.

Safrai, S., and D. Flusser. "The Slave of Two Masters." *Immanuel* 6 (1976), 30–33.

Safrai, S., M. Stern, D. Flusser, and W. C. van Unnik, eds. *The Jewish People in the First Century.* 9 vols. Amsterdam: Van Gorcum, 1974–93.

Safrai, S. "Teaching of Pietists in Mishnaic Literature," *Journal of Jewish Studies* 16 (1965), 15–33.

Sanders, E. P. *Jesus and Judaism.* London: SCM, 1985.

_____. *Jewish Law from Jesus to the Mishnah.* Philadelphia: Trinity, 1990.

_____. *Paul and Palestinian Judaism.* London: SCM, 1977.

Sanders, J. A. *The Psalms Scroll of Qumran Cave 11.* New York: Oxford, 1965.

Sanders, J. T. "First Corinthians 13: Its Interpretation since the First World War," *Interpretation* 20 (1966), 159–87.

Sandmel, Samuel. *The Genius of Paul.* Philadelphia: Fortress, 1979.

_____. *Judaism and Christian Beginnings.* New York: Oxford University Press, 1978.

Schäfer, Peter. *Die Vorstellung vom Heiligen Geist in der rabbinischen Literatur.* Munich: Köstel, 1972.

Schechter, S. *Aspects of Rabbinic Theology.* New York: Schocken, 1961.

_____. *Studies in Judaism.* Philadelphia: Jewish Publication Society, 1896.

Schillebeeckx, E. *Paul the Apostle.* New York: Crossroad, 1983.

Schoeps, H. J. *Paul: The Theology of the Apostle in the Light of Jewish Religious History.* Philadelphia: Westminster, 1961.

Schürer, E. *The History of the Jewish People.* 6 vols. 1891. Reprint. Peabody, Mass.: Hendrickson, 1993.

_____. *The History of the Jewish People.* 3 vols. Revised and edited by G. Vermes, F. Millar, and M. Black. Edinburgh: T. & T. Clark, 1974–87.

Segal, Alan. *Paul the Convert.* New Haven: Yale University Press, 1990.

Sigal, Phillip. *The Halakah of Jesus of Nazareth.* Lanham, Md.: University Press of America, 1986.

Sokoloff, M. *A Dictionary of Jewish Palestinian Aramaic.* Ramat Gan, Israel: Bar Ilan University Press, 1990.

Soloveitchik, Joseph B., *Halachic Man.* Philadelphia: Jewish Publication Society, 1983.

Stendhal, John. "With Luther/Against Luther." *Explorations* 9/3 (1995), 7.

Stendahl, K. *Paul among Jews and Gentiles.* Philadelphia: Fortress, 1976.

_____. *The Scrolls and the New Testament.* New York: Harper, 1957.

Strack, H. *Einleitung in Talmud und Midrasch.* Revised by G. Stemberger. Munich: C. H. Beck, 1981.

_____. *Introduction to the Talmud and Midrash.* Atheneum: New York, 1978 (this English translation was done before Stemberger's revision and now an English translation of G. Stemberger is available, Edinburgh: T. & T. Clark, 1989).

Swete, H. B. *The Gospel according to St. Mark.* London: Macmillan, 1905.

Taylor, V. *The Gospel according to St. Mark.* London: Macmillan, 1941.

_____. *The Text of the New Testament: A Short Introduction.* London: Macmillan, 1961.

Thoma, C. *A Christian Theology of Judaism.* Mahwah: Paulist, 1980.

Titus, E. L. "Did Paul Write I Corinthians 13?" *Journal of Bible and Religion* 27 (1959), 299–302.

Tomson, Peter J. *Paul and the Jewish Law.* Assen: Van Gorcum, 1990.

Unnik, W. C. van. *Tarsus or Jerusalem.* London: Epworth, 1962.

Urbach, E. E. *The Sages: Their Concepts and Beliefs.* 2 vols. Jerusalem: Magnes, 1975.

_____. "Matay Paskah Hanevuah?" *Tarbitz* 17 (1945–46), 1–11.

Vermes, G. *Jesus the Jew.* Glasgow: William Collins & Sons, 1977.

———. *Jesus and the World of Judaism.* London: SCM Press, 1983.

———. *The Religion of Jesus the Jew.* Minneapolis: Fortress, 1993.

———. "Sectarian Matrimonial Halakhah in the Damascus Rule," *Journal of Semitic Studies* 25 (1974), 197ff.

Visotzky, Burton. *Reading the Book: Making the Bible a Timeless Text.* Garden City: Doubleday, 1991.

Weinfeld, Moshe. "Pentecost as Festival of the Giving of the Law." *Immanuel* 8 (1978), 7–18.

Wenham, David. *Paul: Follower of Jesus or Founder of Christianity?* Grand Rapids: Eerdmans, 1995.

Willis, W. *The Kingdom of God in 20th Century Interpretation.* Peabody, Mass.: Hendrickson, 1987.

Wilson, Marvin. *Our Father Abraham.* Grand Rapids: Eerdmans, 1989.

Wilson, R. McL. "Marcion," *The Encyclopedia of Philosophy.* New York: Macmillan, 1972. 5.155f.

Winter, Paul. *On the Trial of Jesus.* Berlin: Walter de Gruyter, 1961.

Wise, M., Norman Golb, J. J. Collins, and D. Pardee. *Methods of Investigation of the Dead Sea Scrolls and the Khirbet Qumran Site.* New York: New York Academy of Sciences, 1994.

Wolpe, David. *Healer of Shattered Hearts: A Jewish View of God.* New York: Henry Holt, 1990.

———. *In Speech and Silence: The Jewish Quest for God.* New York: Henry Holt, 1992.

Young, Brad H. "The Ascension Motif of 2 Corinthians in Jewish, Christian and Gnostic Texts," *Grace Theological Journal* 9,1 (1988), 73–103.

———. "The Cross, Jesus and the Jewish People," *Immanuel* 24–25 (1990), 23–34.

———. *The Jewish Background to the Lord's Prayer.* Austin: Center for Judaic-Christian Studies, 1984.

———. *Jesus and His Jewish Parables.* New York: Paulist, 1989.

Young, Brad H. with David Flusser. "Messianic Blessings in Jewish and Christian Texts." In *Judaism and the Origins of Christianity.* Jerusalem: Magnes, 1989. Pages 280–300.

INDEX OF ANCIENT SOURCES

INDEX OF NAMES AND SUBJECTS

GOSHEN COLLEGE - GOOD LIBRARY

3 9310 01009109 6

DATE DUE

JAN 0 8 1999		
JAN 2 8 1999		
MAR 1 3 2000		
APR 0 4 2000		
APR 2 8 2000		
JAN 2 8 2001		
FEB 1 1 2001		
MAR 1 9 2001		
APR 1 1 2001		
APR 1 7 20		
3/19/03		
GAYLORD		PRINTED IN U.S.A